Childcraft
The How and Why Library

Volume 10

Places to Know

World Book–Childcraft International, Inc.

Chicago London Paris Rome Sydney Tokyo Toronto

Acknowledgments

The publishers of *Childcraft—The How and Why Library*
gratefully acknowledge the courtesy of the
following publishers, agencies, and corporations. Full
illustration acknowledgments for this volume appear
on pages 358–359.

Curtis Publishing Co.: photography by Arnold Newman,
page 149, copyright by Curtis Publishing Co.

Sawyer's Inc.: models and photography, pages 6–18,
and Heritage binding cover,
copyright by Sawyer's, Inc., 1962.

Time Inc.: photography pages 272–273 by Robert Capa,
Magnum, courtesy *Life* magazine.

Volume 10

Places to Know

Contents

PLACES TO KNOW

Tell me about all kinds of places!

Faraway places and places near home:
Old places, new places,
glad places, sad places,
rich places, poor places,
highlands and lowlands,
oceans and rivers,
mountains and valleys,
quaint places, spooky places,
curious places.

This book will tell you about many places to know all over the world.

If you stop to think about it, television, telephones, and jet planes are some of the wonders in our world today.

Today, we know about seven wonders of the ancient world because men have found writings, drawings, and pieces of them.

What did people think was so wonderful long ago— and why did they think so? You can find out in the next pages.

All photographs in this section are of small-scale models constructed by the Creative Studios of Sawyer's Inc., Portland, Oregon.

NO WONDER I'M A WONDER

I was once a statue named Colossus. I was made of bronze. I stood beside the harbor of a small island called Rhodes in the Aegean Sea.

I was twenty times taller than a man, and my thumb was so big that you couldn't even wrap your arms around it. If you could have stood on my head, you could have seen far out across land and sea.

Why was I built? Well, long ago, the people of Rhodes tried to save their island in a battle against thousands of men from another land. They had little hope of winning, but the men and women fought hard. Finally, the courage of the islanders was rewarded when their friend, Ptolemy, came to their aid with a powerful fleet of ships and saved Rhodes.

The Rhodians were so grateful to be saved that they built me in honor of their victory. I stood in the harbor for many years. Poets wrote about my beauty, and they called me one of the Seven Wonders of the World. The word "colossal" comes from my name.

One day, the earth began to tremble and quake. The trembling was so ferocious that I tumbled down and fell apart and couldn't be put back together.

Today, I am just a statue called the Colossus of Rhodes that you read about in books. But, every once in a while, men find bits and pieces of the bronze that used to be part of me.

7

WHERE
A GODDESS LIVED

Long ago, the people of Greece and Rome believed in many gods and goddesses. Stories, which we call myths, were made up about the gods and goddesses. These myths helped to explain the things in nature that the people did not understand. The myths also told of special powers the gods and goddesses had to help or harm others.

One of the goddesses was the protector of wild animals. People in Greece called her Artemis. People in Rome called her Diana. The Greeks built a temple to honor her, and they put a statue of her inside the temple. The temple was made of white marble and glittered with gold. It was so large that some said it "rose to the clouds."

The Temple of Artemis was built more than 2,500 years ago. It took many years to build. When it was finished, people traveled great distances to see this wonder. Then the temple was destroyed by fire. But people loved the goddess so much, they built an even fancier temple in the same place.

Years and years later, enemy soldiers burned down the temple. It was never rebuilt. Even though the Temple of Artemis is gone, you can read about it in many books—even the Bible. Today, you can see the ruins of the temple at Ephesus in the country of Turkey.

THE GREAT STONE TENT

Cheops was the name of a king in ancient Egypt who wanted a place to stay when he died. So, he ordered his men to build a huge stone house in the shape of a pyramid. A pyramid looks somewhat like an enormous tent. The base of this pyramid is almost large enough to fill ten football fields. Its peak is as high as a stairway with more than eight hundred stairs.

How did the men build the pyramid? They didn't have trucks, cranes, or bulldozers to help them. Each stone weighed as much as four cows. How did the men lift these giant stones to the top of the pyramid? Maybe the men pulled the giant stones up a ramp on sleds as you see in the picture. Nobody really knows. But we do know that the pyramid took twenty years to build.

Today, we could build the Great Pyramid in less than a year.

The Great Pyramid still stands in Egypt, and people come from all over the world to see the great wonder that was built more than four thousand years ago—the only ancient wonder of the world still standing.

HANGING GARDENS

A long time ago, King Nebuchadnezzar lived in a land called Babylonia. He married a beautiful princess from another land and brought her to Babylon, the capital of Babylonia. The new queen grew homesick for the mountains and gardens of her country.

So the king called together his architects and craftsmen to plan the most beautiful gardens the world had ever seen.

The work began. The king's men built tall walls and terraces, and there they put in flowers, fruit trees, and fountains. The gardens were the highest anyone had ever seen. They were as high as a building with thirty-five stories.

Building the gardens wasn't easy without machinery. Men had to haul rocks and stones from far away to build the walls and terraces and fountains.

And to keep the gardens green and the fountains flowing, they had to pump water in from a faraway river.

We don't know for certain that this story is true, but we do know from old writings that the Hanging Gardens of Babylon did exist.

In the country of Iraq, men called archaeologists have found empty wells, ditches, and cellars which must have once been part of the Hanging Gardens of Babylon. The word "hanging" is confusing because the gardens did not really hang. "Hanging" may have come from a Latin word that meant balconies and terraces. The picture shows how one artist imagined this wonder of the ancient world.

WHO'S ZEUS?

Thousands of years ago, people believed that a god named Zeus watched over the sky and the weather.

A Greek sculptor and his men carved a statue of Zeus at a place called Olympia in Greece. No one had ever seen a statue this large made entirely of ivory and gold. Zeus sat on a throne and was so big that if you had stood on his shoulder, you'd have had to stretch to peek into his ear.

Some said that just one glance at Zeus would cause you to forget all your troubles.

Once every four years, the people around Olympia had a festival to honor Zeus. Today, more than two thousand years later, nations still meet every four years—for the Olympic Games.

The giant statue of Zeus is gone. But men of that time wrote descriptions of it, and from the descriptions, artists have drawn pictures and made models of it.

A LIGHT
IN THE NIGHT

Crack! Thunder fills the night. The rough sea rocks and tosses the ships sailing toward Alexandria, a city in Egypt. But the sailors are not worried. They can see in the distance the bright flames at the top of the lighthouse. The light guides their ships toward the island of Pharos in the city's harbor. Soon, they are safely home.

The lighthouse the sailors saw was known as the Pharos of Alexandria. One of the seven wonders of the ancient world, it was more than 400 feet (122 meters) high. At its base was a 300-room fortress where soldiers could fight off approaching enemies. A bonfire burned continuously at the top of the tower.

The Pharos of Alexandria, built about 2,300 years ago, guided sailors to safety for more than a thousand years. But then Arabs destroyed part of it searching for gold that wasn't there. Later, an earthquake destroyed more of it. Finally, about 700 years ago, another earthquake toppled it into the sea. The great Pharos of Alexandria was no more.

HORSES ON THE ROOF

If you had lived a few thousand years ago, you could have taken a ride in a four-horse chariot like the one on top of this building.

The building was the famous gold and marble tomb of a king named Mausolus. It may be that Mausolus and his queen were the people riding in the chariot.

When the king died, his queen ordered a tomb for him that would be known and admired all over the world. The name Mausolus lives today in our language in the word "mausoleum." A mausoleum is the name we use for a burial tomb above the ground.

The tomb of Mausolus was built in an ancient city called Halicarnassus which is now the city of Bodrum in Turkey. The tomb was destroyed. But you can see part of the chariot group that was saved, if you visit the British Museum in London, England.

SAHARA

PIRANHA

MT. EVEREST

VERRAZANO BRIDGE

If you see fireworks bursting in the sky, you might say, ''Oh!'' And if you see a litter of puppies, you might say, ''Ah!''

Other times you might feel like saying ''Oh'' or ''Ah'' are when you see certain places in the world—the river with enough water to cover a country, the building so high that you can make shadow pictures on the clouds it pokes through, the volcano that grew up in a farmer's field, and the ocean of sand that once may have been an ocean of water.

You can find out about these places on the next few pages.

Many smaller rivers join the mighty Amazon as it nears the Atlantic Ocean.

The Amazon River is so wide, the people living in this village can hardly see the other side.

WHAT A RIVER!

The Amazon River is the biggest river in the world. It contains more water than the Nile, the Mississippi, and the Yangtze rivers put together. And next to the Nile, it is the longest river in the world. The Amazon starts in Peru and slowly flows all the way across Brazil to the Atlantic Ocean. Over most of this great distance, the river flows through jungles where it rains for months at a time.

The surface of the Amazon looks as smooth as glass. But under the surface, the water is full of snakes, eels, alligators, and a deadly fish called the piranha. These tiny fish attack in bunches. They can eat an animal as big as a horse in just a few minutes.

There's a lot of life on the surface of the Amazon River, too. Some of the people living along the river build their houses on wooden rafts that are tied together with ropes. Then, when the river floods during the rainy season, the whole village rises with the water.

SHOWER FOR A GIANT OR TWO

The Niagara Falls are two falls.
The American Falls are on the left in this picture, and the Horseshoe Falls in Canada are on the right.

Niagara Falls would be a great place for a giant to take a shower. In fact, two giants could take a shower at Niagara Falls because there are two Niagara Falls. That's because the Niagara River splits. Part of the water of the river runs over Horseshoe Falls in Canada. The rest of the water runs over the American Falls in the state of New York.

You're not as tall as a giant, but you can go right up to the falls. You go in a steamboat called *The Maid of the Mist*.

As the boat gets close to the falls, the roar of the falling water is so loud that you have to shout to be heard. And you can see that the water breaks into tiny drops of mist as it thunders over the falls. If you look up from the deck of *The Maid of the Mist* at the right time, you can see the sun making a bright rainbow above the falls.

GREAT GUSHING GEYSERS!

A geyser shoots water like a fountain. But a geyser shoots steaming hot water from a hole deep in the ground. Some geysers shoot water high into the air. Others just bubble up from the ground. Some geysers may go off several times in an hour. Others may be quiet for years.

Groups of geysers are found in different parts of the world. In the far north, in Iceland, there's a group of geysers about an hour's drive from the city of Reykjavík. It's from one of the geysers in this group—the *Stori Geysir*—that we get the word "geyser." This word comes from the Old Icelandic *geysa,* which means "to gush."

Far to the south, on the other side of the world, there is another large group of geysers in New Zealand. Both New Zealand and Iceland make electricity with the steam from geysers and hot springs.

Perhaps the most famous geyser in the world is "Old Faithful," in Yellowstone National Park, Wyoming. It is one of a group of about two hundred active geysers. "Old Faithful" erupts for about four minutes once every hour. And it has not missed once in the more than eighty years people have kept track of it!

Children at Strokkur, Iceland, watch a geyser
shoot hot water high into the air.

THE ROYAL GORGE WAR

Long ago, two railroad companies had a fight about a big ditch in the Rocky Mountains. The big ditch is in Colorado, and its name is the Royal Gorge.

It used to be that the only way to get to the silver mines near the top of the mountains was through the Royal Gorge. So the railroad companies began to fight to see which one would build its tracks through the gorge. They had quite a problem. The gorge is almost a quarter of a mile (0.5 kilometer) deep, and the bottom is so narrow in some places that there seemed to be no room for anything but the river running through the gorge.

One company started building railroad tracks in the middle of the gorge. All the men and tools had to be lowered over the sides with ropes. Then the other company blockaded one end of the gorge. Both companies built forts and hired many cowboys and gunslingers.

During the day, the railroad crews worked to lay the tracks. At night, they rolled boulders down the sides of the gorge to smash each other's tracks. They dumped each other's tools in the river. They even used dynamite to wreck each other's work.

Finally, the owners of the two railroad companies met and talked things over. And one company agreed to sell its tracks so that the railroad could be finished.

If you ever visit Royal Gorge, you can get a good look at the railroad from the Royal Gorge Bridge. The Royal Gorge Bridge hangs across the top of the gorge and is the highest suspension bridge in the world.

The Royal Gorge Bridge in Colorado is the highest suspension bridge in the world. ▶

THE SMOKE THAT THUNDERS

One of the most beautiful waterfalls in the world is on the Zambezi River in Africa. At the river's halfway point, between the countries of Zambia and Rhodesia, the water plunges over Victoria Falls. These falls are often listed as one of the seven natural wonders of the world. At the falls, the river is about a mile (1.5 kilometers) wide. And at the highest point, it falls 355 feet (108 meters) into a rocky canyon. The falling water sounds like thunder. The huge clouds of spray look like thick white smoke.

The local people called the falls "Musi-oa-tunya" which means "the smoke that thunders." That was before explorer David Livingstone saw the falls for the first time, more than a hundred years ago. He named them after Queen Victoria of Great Britain.

In Zambia, close to the falls, there's a hotel that keeps the old name—the Musi-o-Tunya. From the hotel you can walk down to the falls to enjoy the unforgettable sight and sound of "the smoke that thunders."

"The ground is hot—almost hot enough to burn my feet! It's been getting hotter every day."

That's what a farmer named Dionisio Pulido thought as he plowed his cornfield near Parícutin, Mexico.

Suddenly, the ground began to shake and crack, and a big puff of smoke and steam roared out of a hole in the ground.

Dionisio ran to the village and warned the people that there was a monster in his cornfield. It wasn't a monster, of course. It was a volcano being born.

It shot ashes and steam and melted rock out of the ground until all of Dionisio's farm was buried.

It grew through the spring and summer until it became higher than the highest building in the world.

It forced people who lived in the village of Parícutin to run away so they wouldn't be buried under it. It grew until it buried another town, too. During the day, the sky was black with falling ashes. And at night, the sky was red with sparks and glowed with melted rock.

The volcano kept growing year after year until it became a mountain. Then, it stopped growing.

Today, Parícutin volcano is quiet. In just ten years, it grew big enough to be counted by some people as one of the seven natural wonders of the world.

Lava from Parícutin almost buried this church tower in a nearby village.

These mountain climbers in the Himalayas were led by Sir Edmund Hillary, the first explorer to climb Mount Everest.

CLIMBING
TO THE TOP OF THE WORLD

If you want to get to the top of the highest mountain in the world, you have to climb as high as a plane flies. There aren't any roads or tracks that reach to the top of the mountain. There isn't even a path or room on top for a plane to land.

The mountain is Mount Everest in the Himalaya range on the border of Nepal and Tibet in Asia.

The only way to get to the top of Mount Everest is to walk, and climb, and crawl there yourself. You have to drive spikes into the rock and cut your own stairs in the ice. One false step and you could be killed in a fall straight down.

When you get to the top of Mount Everest, you're about five and a half miles (9 kilometers) high. On a clear day, you can see many other mountain peaks against the blue sky. The air doesn't have enough oxygen for you to breathe. So you have to take tanks of oxygen with you.

Mount Everest is the highest mountain in the world.

A GIANT OF A BUILDING

It reaches skyward like a mighty giant. It has 110 stories and is 1,454 feet (443 meters) high. This giant of a building is Sears Tower, in Chicago, Illinois. It is the tallest building in the world.

Just to plan Sears Tower took about three years. Then it took four years and millions of dollars to build. The building looks like nine towers—of different heights—all clustered together.

To handle the crowds of workers and visitors, Sears Tower has seven lobbies and more than a hundred elevators. Four of the lobbies are so high up they're called sky-lobbies. These sky-lobbies are served by double-deck elevators—two elevators built one on top of the other. Each elevator has room for 25 people. When these double-deck elevators stop, the top elevator is at one floor and the bottom elevator is at the floor below. This happens in the sky-lobbies on the 33rd and 34th floors and the 66th and 67th floors.

You can ride in one of two elevators that zoom up to the Skydeck on the 103rd floor. The trip takes less than a minute. From the observation deck, you can get a giant's eyeview of Chicago and the surrounding area.

Sears Tower, in Chicago, Illinois, is the tallest building in the world.

LAKE IN THE SKY

If you were an Uru, you'd be an Indian. And you'd live on an island—but not just any kind of an island. It would be an island that you, yourself, would make of bundles of reeds.

You'd float your island on a lake—but not just any kind of a lake. It would be the highest lake in the world that anyone can travel on.

What's more, you'd build your own hut out of reeds. You'd build your own boat out of reeds, too. You'd go fishing for trout in the morning —and probably wear earmuffs at the same time because the mountain air is so cold. In bad weather, your island would shimmy and shake. But you wouldn't mind. You'd be used to living that way, and you'd tell visitors that your ancestors were older than the sun.

You'd be living on Lake Titicaca in the Andes Mountains in South America, between the countries of Peru and Bolivia.

Indians live on Lake Titicaca in the Andes Mountains of South America and travel in boats made of reeds.

AN OCEAN OF SAND

You'd never expect to find skeletons of fish in the Sahara desert in Africa. But scientists have found them there.

Long ago, the Sahara desert may have been an ocean of water. If that is true, the fish bones were left behind when the water dried up. But, before the water dried up, something else may have happened. A huge garden with rivers and fields of grass may have grown where the desert is now. Drawings found on the walls of caves in the desert show animals that couldn't have lived in a desert.

After a long time, the rivers dried up. So did the grass. And what may have been first an ocean, and then a garden, became the biggest desert in the world.

Prehistoric men carved the drawings on this rock in the Sahara desert.

SIMÓN BOLÍVAR

IVAN THE TERRIBLE

THEODORE ROOSEVELT

The club you may belong to has rules or laws. So do governments.

But the people who run governments don't meet in a basement or a clubhouse the way your club might. Instead, they meet in special places in cities called capitals. Some government leaders meet in buildings on hills. Some meet in buildings on an island, and the leaders of at least one government meet in a museum.

On the following pages, you will visit places where governments are run in different parts of the world.

NAMING THE WHITE HOUSE

George Washington chose the place where the house of the President of the United States was built in Washington, D.C. From time to time, this famous house has been repaired and rebuilt. Even though this has changed its appearance, the outside of the house has always been painted white. That's why it was known as the "white house" long before the name became official.

For many years it was called the "President's House," and even the "President's Palace." After the Civil War, it became known as the "Executive Mansion." Finally, in 1901, when Theodore Roosevelt was President, the official name was changed to the "White House."

The President and his family live in the White House. There are also offices for the President and many of the people who work with him. The lawmakers in Congress, who help the President run the government, work in another building called the United States Capitol.

The United States Capitol is where the members of Congress meet.

The White House is where the President of the United States of America lives.

Senators meet in the senate chamber of the Parliament Buildings in Ottawa.

UP THE HILL

If the flag flies during the day, it means that they're meeting. But, if a red light shines at the top of the flagpole at night, it means they've gone home.

Who are they? They are the lawmakers of Canada. One group of lawmakers are members of the House of Commons. They are called commoners. The other group of lawmakers are members of the Senate. They are called senators. The commoners and senators meet in the Parliament Buildings on Parliament Hill in the city of Ottawa.

One of the Parliament Buildings has a tall tower that's known as the Peace Tower. That's where the flag flies and the light shines. The Peace Tower also has a big clock and many bells. The smallest bell weighs about as much as a newborn baby, and the largest weighs more than three newborn whales. Sometimes songs are played on the bells. But no matter how many songs are played, the last two are always "O Canada" and "God Save the Queen."

Canadian guardsmen march in front of the Peace Tower in Ottawa. ▶

44   Queen Elizabeth II of England opens a session of Parliament.

A PALACE FOR LAWMAKERS

There is a palace
where you could have a lot of fun playing.
It has a hundred stairways to climb,
passageways to run through,
and a tall clock tower to hide in.
But it's not a palace for playing.
It's the New Palace of Westminster
in London, England,
and it's a palace for lawmaking.

Not many people know that its real name is the New Palace of
Westminster because almost everyone knows it as the Houses of
Parliament. The English lawmakers who meet there are called
members of the Parliament.

One of the best known parts of the Houses of Parliament is Big
Ben. Big Ben is the name of a famous bell that rings with a deep
bong. It's inside a huge clock tower, and the clock itself is so big
that the minute hand is as long as a diving board.

At night, if you see a light on the Clock Tower, you know that the
members of Parliament are meeting.

The Houses of Parliament in London, England,
are beside the river Thames.
Big Ben is in the tower with the clock.

GOVERNMENT IN A MUSEUM

You might expect to find barracks for soldiers behind the walls of a fortress. But would you also expect to find palaces, and cathedrals, and even some government buildings there, too?

Such buildings stand behind the walls of one fortress—the Kremlin in Moscow, the capital of Russia. "Kremlin" comes from a Russian word that means "fortress."

You can't visit the government buildings in the Kremlin because they're secret. But you can visit such places as the Armory Palace and see many things that once belonged to czars. Czars were the emperors of Russia long ago.

In the Armory, you can see jeweled Easter eggs, golden helmets, guns and armor, jeweled sabers, and even the throne of the czar named Ivan the Terrible.

This is the Kremlin in Moscow, Russia.
The red star is on top of the Kremlin Tower,
and the red flag is on top of the Grand Palace.

Andorra's capital city lies in a beautiful mountain valley.

THE PRINCES OF ANDORRA

Once upon a time, a Spanish nobleman decided to give his country away. The tiny country he ruled was Andorra, high up in the Pyrenees Mountains between Spain and France. The nobleman gave his country to a Spanish bishop. So, for a couple of hundred years, Spanish bishops ruled Andorra.

But one day, the ruling bishop decided he couldn't defend the tiny country. He asked a Spanish nobleman to help. Then, members of the Spanish nobleman's family married into a noble French family. Before long, one of the French noblemen decided he wanted to rule Andorra.

The Spanish bishop disagreed. How did they settle the matter? They both became princes of Andorra and ruled the tiny country together! But they let the people elect a General Council to make some local laws. And that's the way it's been ever since. The General Council meets in the House of the Valleys, in Andorra, the capital city.

Today, the princes of Andorra are the president of France and the bishop of Lerida, Spain. According to custom, one year the people of Andorra give the French president a gift of about $200. The next year they give the Spanish bishop about $8. But every year the bishop also gets 6 hams, 12 rounds of cheese, 12 capons, and 12 partridges. He gives the food to needy people in Spain.

The lawmakers of Andorra meet in the House of the Valleys.

49

Behind the lion in this picture is the old parliament building in Stockholm, Sweden.

Stockholm, the capital of Sweden, is built on many islands that are connected by bridges.

GOVERNMENT ON AN ISLAND

You can cross a lot of bridges in Stockholm, Sweden—so many that some people call Stockholm the City of Bridges. Stockholm needs bridges because it's built on a dozen islands along the coast of Sweden.

The lawmakers of Sweden use one of the bridges to get to work on one of the islands. These lawmakers are called the Riksdag, and their meeting place is called the Riksdagshuset. If the lawmakers have to go to the bank, they don't have to go very far. The oldest government-owned bank in the world—the Riksbank—stands near the Riksdagshuset.

51

AUSTRALIA'S MEETING PLACE

Less than a hundred years ago, Australia was made up of six separate colonies. These colonies were ruled by the British. Then, in 1901, the colonies united to form the Commonwealth of Australia.

Today, Australia is an independent country. But it is also a member of the Commonwealth of Nations. This is a group of countries that were once under British rule. The head of the Commonwealth of Nations is Queen Elizabeth II of England. This also makes her queen of Australia. But the queen doesn't rule the Australians. They vote for their own lawmakers, who meet in Parliament House in Canberra, the capital city.

The name Canberra comes from the Aboriginal word *kamberri,* which means "meeting place." When it was chosen as the capital, this beautiful "meeting place" had few trees. As part of an experiment, oaks, elms, beeches, birches, cottonwoods, firs, and cypresses were brought in from other parts of the world. But the people also wanted native Australian trees. One kind they planted was the gum tree, which is their name for the eucalyptus. They also put in many acacias, known as wattles in Australia.

The wattle and gum tree are especially important because they are among Australia's unofficial emblems. In fact, flowering branches of wattle form the background of Australia's coat of arms. In all, more than one and a half million trees and shrubs were planted to make Australia's capital more beautiful.

The National Diet Building in Tokyo is where the parliament of Japan meets.

THE RULERS OF JAPAN

For more than two thousand years, Japan was ruled by emperors, or by people who ruled for the emperor. During all this time, the Japanese honored their emperor as a god. According to legend, the emperors were related to the sun goddess, Amaterasu.

But after World War II, Emperor Hirohito said this belief was false. Then the people voted for leaders to run their country. The Japanese still honor the emperor, but he has no power. He is the symbol of the country and the people.

The emperor and his family live in the Imperial Palace in Tokyo, the capital of Japan. Ordinary people can visit the palace only twice a year—the day after New Year and on the birthday of the emperor.

The palace is surrounded by a moat—a wide, water-filled ditch. To get to the palace, you must cross a heavy stone bridge over the moat. Sometimes you see white swans swimming in the moat.

Close to the grounds of the Imperial Palace is the National Diet Building. "Diet" means parliament. The people who are elected to the Diet make the laws for Japan. They also choose the prime minister, who is now the "ruler" of Japan.

A stone bridge over a moat leads to the Imperial Palace.

Rio de Janeiro used to be the capital of Brazil. Now the capital of Brazil is Brasília.

GOODBYE, RIO—HELLO

For many years, the government of Brazil was run from Rio de Janeiro— a city that's so beautiful that its harbor is considered by many to be one of the seven natural wonders of the world.

But, not long ago, the government of Brazil decided to build a new capital in the wilderness. Workers cleared the land and built modern buildings of concrete slabs and glass. Some buildings are built on columns over pools of water so the buildings look as though they're floating. The workers even dug out a long lake that borders the new city called Brasília.

The lawmakers of Brazil hoped that many people would move to the new capital. Instead, many of the people who work in Brasília can hardly wait for the weekend. That's when they go back to the old capital city Rio de Janeiro.

57

CITY IN A CITY

The lawmakers of Israel had no place of their own to meet. So they did something about it. They built a new city in the city of Jerusalem and called it Government City.

Besides government buildings, Government City has several museums. The Israel Museum is where the Dead Sea Scrolls are kept. If you want to see the Dead Sea Scrolls, you have to go to a special building most of which is under the ground. The building is called the Shrine of the Book. The Book is the Bible. The scrolls are the oldest writings of the Bible ever found. They were discovered not long ago in caves near the Dead Sea. The most important scroll is the Book of Isaiah. If it's ever in any kind of danger, all someone has to do is press a button, and the Book of Isaiah disappears into a special vault.

The white dome of the Shrine of the Book rises above the underground building.

For thousands of years, people have built places where they can pray and worship. Jews build synagogues, Moslems build mosques, Christians build churches, and Buddhists build temples.

The next pages will show you places of worship where people of different religions pray.

The huge dome of Saint Peter's Church in Vatican City
looks like this when you look up at it from inside.

THE DISAPPEARING TOE
AT SAINT PETER'S

Your big toe might wear away, too, if people kissed it every day for years and years and years.

That's what has happened to the big toe of a bronze statue of Saint Peter. The statue sits on a throne in a famous church called Saint Peter's Church in Vatican City, Italy. Many people visit Saint Peter's every year, and thousands of people have leaned down to kiss or touch the foot of the statue in memory of the great saint. So many kisses have made its toe wear away.

Many people say that the tomb of Saint Peter rests under the main altar of Saint Peter's Church. Crowning the tomb, high above the altar, is a famous dome, or roof, that seems to rise toward the sky.

After you enter the church, you can see the statue of Saint Peter with its worn-away toe.

This is the bronze statue with the disappearing toe.

THE REAL MECCA

If you want to be a *hajji*, you have to make a *hajj*.

A *hajj* is a pilgrimage, or journey, to the city of Mecca in Saudi Arabia. Moslems, as believers in the religion of Islam are called, try to make a *hajj* once in their life. After a Moslem makes a *hajj* to the holy city of Mecca, he is called a *hajji*, or pilgrim.

The Great Mosque, or place of prayer, in Mecca is the center of worship for all Moslems. Near the Great Mosque is a small building shaped like a box. It is called the Kaaba. The Kaaba holds the sacred Black Stone that Moslems believe God sent from heaven. Wherever Moslems live, they face in the direction of the Kaaba when they pray.

Today, we use the word "mecca" to mean a place many people visit—a mecca for children could be a zoo, a park, or an ice-cream shop. But the real Mecca is the holy city for Moslems.

A HOLY CITY
FOR HINDUS

The city of Banaras, India, has more than a thousand places to pray—temples for people who belong to the Hindu religion.

Most Hindu temples have many shrines. Hindus go to these shrines to pray. Each temple has a main shrine for one important god or goddess. One of the most visited temples is the Temple of Siva. The god Siva is one of the three most important gods. The other two are Brahma and Vishnu.

About a million Hindus visit the holy city of Banaras every year. They come from all over India. Before praying in the temples, pilgrims go down the *ghats,* or stairways, into the Ganges River. They believe that if they bathe in the river, they will wash away their sins. The sick and the crippled go into the river hoping the water will cure them.

All Hindus believe that if their dead bodies or ashes are placed in the river, the Ganges will carry them to eternal happiness.

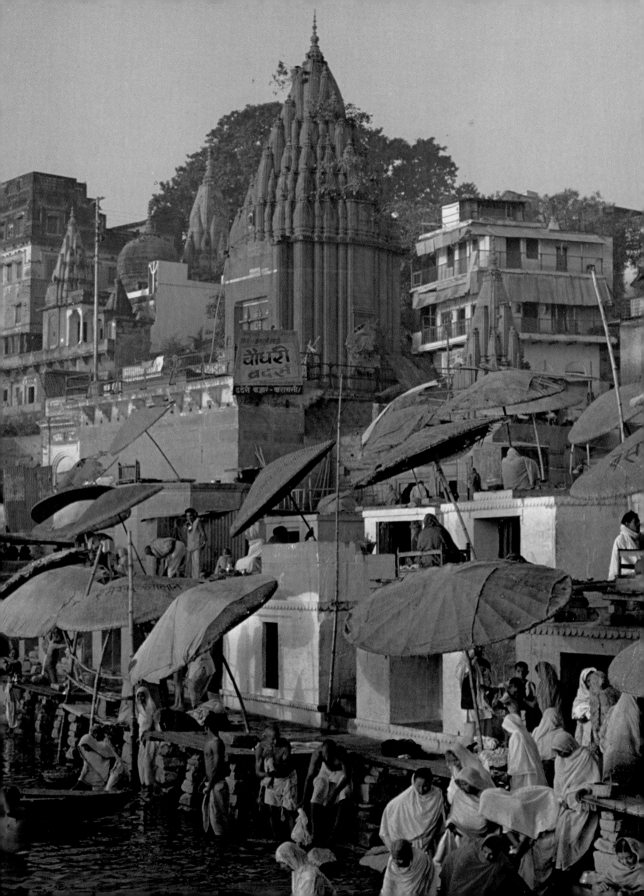

The golden building is a shrine to Buddha. It is in Rangoon, Burma.

HAIR FOR HONEY

Once, there lived a man who was a great teacher and doctor. People thought that he was so wise that they gave him the title Buddha, which means "The Enlightened One."

It is said that during Buddha's life, two brothers named Poo and Taupau visited Buddha and gave him a gift of honey. Then, they asked Buddha if he would give them some little thing, in the same way you might ask a famous person for his autograph. Buddha plucked eight hairs from his head and gave them to the brothers. Poo and Taupau then built a shrine to Buddha.

Today, if you visit Rangoon in a country called Burma, you can see what some people consider the most beautiful shrine to Buddha in the world. It is called the Shwe Dagon Pagoda. The top of the pagoda looks like a giant golden bell, and Buddhists say that it contains the eight precious hairs of Buddha, who lived more than two thousand years ago.

These are some of the many statues of Buddha inside the golden shrine at Rangoon, Burma.

THE MOST SACRED
SHRINE FOR JEWS

Strong voices ring out in song as other voices join in prayer. It's Friday evening in the Old City of Jerusalem, and the Sabbath, a holy day for people of the Jewish faith, is beginning.

The people sing and pray before their most sacred shrine. In Hebrew, this shrine is called the Western Wall. That's just what it is—the western wall of an ancient courtyard.

A glorious Temple once stood inside the courtyard. The Temple was destroyed and rebuilt more than once. Finally, only part of the western wall remained. Then the Jews were driven from their homeland. Many years passed before they could return to stay. But the Temple was never rebuilt.

Jews come from all over the world to pray at the wall. Many write prayers and messages on pieces of paper. They place the papers in small openings in the wall. They also wail, or cry, for the loss of their Temple. That's why the wall has come to be known as the Wailing Wall.

Jews pray before the Wailing Wall in Jerusalem.
Men wear either a hat or *yarmulka* to show respect for God.

The building with the rounded roof is the Mormon Tabernacle. It stands next to the Mormon Temple in Salt Lake City, Utah.

NO ECHOES

If you talk or sing before an audience, and your voice echoes, the echo makes your words bump into each other. That's bad, because people can't understand what you're saying or singing.

Great musicians of the world like to sing and play in places that don't have echoes. When a violinist plucks once on his violin string, he wants to hear "plunk" not "plunk, plunk."

Men who design auditoriums and opera houses study a science called acoustics (you say: uh KOOS ticks). The study of acoustics helps men know about sound and how to control it.

One place known for its good acoustics is a church called the Mormon Tabernacle in Salt Lake City, Utah.

The tabernacle's roof looks like an upside-down bowl. Large timbers were cut or bent to make the roof curve. The builders fastened the timbers together with large wooden pins.

If you drop a needle on the floor at one end of the Mormon Tabernacle, people can hear the "plink" at the opposite end. That's good acoustics!

Maybe that's why so many people enjoy hearing the famous organ and choir in the Mormon Tabernacle.

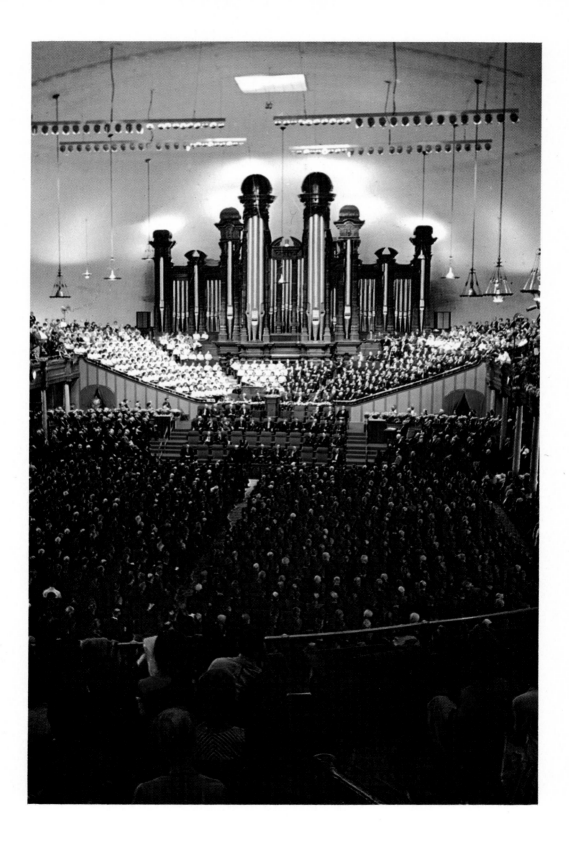

GIFT OF STONE

Before the temple in this picture was built near Chicago, Illinois, a man from Persia (now called Iran) arrived to mark the place where the temple would rise. Some people say that as a small group of people gathered around him for the ceremony, a woman appeared with a little, red wagon that held a large stone. The man from Persia took her gift and used it to mark the spot where the temple would be.

That temple is called the Bahá'í House of Worship (say: bah HAH ee). It was named for a man called Bahá'u'lláh, who was the founder of the Bahá'í religion.

If you visit the famous temple, you can see the gift of the stone enshrined inside.

This winter scene shows the Bahá'í House of Worship near Chicago, Illinois.

This view of Istanbul, Turkey, includes the Hagia Sophia, the largest building on the left.

A CHURCH MUSEUM

If you become a famous soldier, you might have a city named for you. That's what happened to a great warrior named Constantine. When he was crowned emperor of the Roman Empire long ago, he left Rome and built a new city called Constantinople. In Constantinople, he built a church called Hagia Sophia which means "Holy Wisdom." Later, another emperor built another church with the same name.

Hagia Sophia was a cathedral of the Eastern Orthodox Church. "Orthodox" comes from the Greek words "orthos" and "doxa" meaning "true belief."

Constantinople, today, is called Istanbul, and Hagia Sophia, which has been both a cathedral and a mosque, is now a museum that overlooks the city. On one wall, you can see a picture of the great Emperor Constantine.

The Greek Orthodox Cathedral called Saint Sophia in Los Angeles, California, resembles the ancient Hagia Sophia in Istanbul.

Some of the walls inside the Hagia Sophia are decorated with colored tiles.

This is one kind of gargoyle.

GARGOYLES IN THE GUTTERS

Is that a monster, or a lion, or a giant bird looking down from the church top?

It's a monster, half-man and half-beast. But it isn't real. It is made of stone and called a gargoyle. It's one of many weird stone figures that decorate the gutters of the Cathedral of Notre Dame in Paris, France. Gargoyle comes from a Latin word that means gullet or drain. That's what gargoyles are—drain pipes. Each gargoyle has a passageway inside that carries rainwater from the roof and out through the gargoyle's mouth.

Notre Dame is an old cathedral that stands on an island in the Seine River in the center of Paris. "Notre Dame" is the way the French say "Our Lady."

Kings and queens were crowned in the cathedral, including the Emperor Napoleon and his Empress Josephine.

The gargoyles have carried rain from the roof of the famous Cathedral of Notre Dame for more than six hundred years.

The Cathedral of Notre Dame in Paris, France

Two gargoyles stick out above the statues alongside the huge rose window in the Cathedral of Notre Dame.

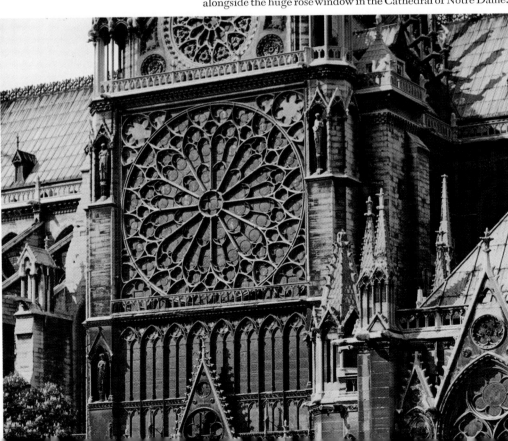

BIBLELAND

The Bible is a sacred book for Jews and Christians. The Christian Bible has two parts—the Old Testament and the New Testament. The Jewish Bible is the Old Testament. The word "bible" comes from a Greek word *biblía* that means books.

Stories in the Bible tell us how people lived, traveled, fought, and worshiped thousands of years ago. If you want to visit the lands described in the Bible, you must travel to the eastern end of the Mediterranean Sea. There you will find many of the places that you read about in the Bible.

You will also find many places of worship. In the city of Jerusalem, for example, Christians can worship at the Church of the Holy Sepulchre. This church is believed to stand on the hill of Calvary, or Golgotha, where Jesus was crucified.

Jews can worship at the Wailing Wall, their most sacred shrine.

Moslems can worship at the Dome of the Rock, which is also known as the Mosque of Omar.

In this view of Jerusalem, the large building is the
Dome of the Rock, just behind the walls of the Old City.
The new sections of Jerusalem rise in the distance.

MEETING HOUSE OF THE WORLD

Today, if two countries of the world have an argument or a fight, an organization called the United Nations is the go-between. The United Nations is a group of people from many nations who work to keep peace in the world.

The United Nations meets at the United Nations Headquarters in New York City. Near the headquarters is a building called The Church Center for the United Nations. People from many church organizations meet at the center to learn about the work of the United Nations.

The picture on this page shows the chapel on the first floor of the center, where people can pray for world peace.

A treasure can be trunks of gold buried by a pirate, or bars of gold buried by a government.

A treasure can be a famous painting hanging on a wall, or a picture painted right on a wall.

Even a building can be a treasure, and so can a piece of paper or an old airplane.

To find out more about treasures such as these, and the places where they are, read the next pages.

BUILDINGS JUST FOR PICTURES

Most buildings are built for people to live in, work in, or go to school in. But some buildings are built just to hang pictures in. These buildings are called art museums. In all parts of the world, cities and towns have art museums to hang pictures in.

You may think of a picture as a decoration for your house, your school, or your father's office. But sometimes pictures are not just decorations. Sometimes they are famous works of art. And, art museums are places where you can go to see works of art that have been painted by famous artists—some who lived long ago and some who are living today.

In the Rijksmuseum in Amsterdam, The Netherlands

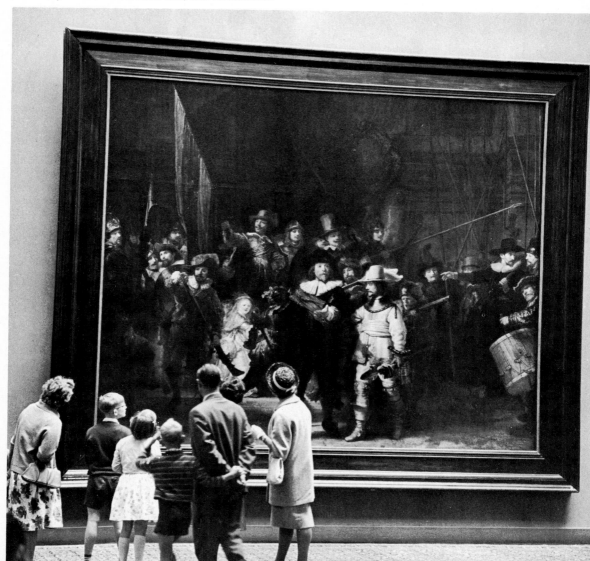

In the Prado museum in Madrid, Spain

In the Metropolitan Museum of Art in New York City

In the Uffizi Gallery in Florence, Italy

FROM FORT
TO PICTURE HOUSE

Once, long ago, a king of France built a fort to protect himself. Many years later, another king of France added more buildings to the fort and turned it into a palace. The halls of the buildings were so big that the king and his son used to ride on horseback in and out of its many hallways. Today, this palace is a house used especially for pictures. Thousands of pictures decorate its walls. Thousands of statues stand on its floors, and thousands of other art treasures are displayed in more than one hundred rooms of the palace.

This gigantic picture house is the Louvre, and it's in Paris, France. No one knows where that name came from, but the Louvre is the largest art museum in the world.

The art is so valuable that during World Wars I and II, the government of France took all the treasures out of the Louvre and hid them. The hiding place is still kept a secret.

Winged Victory, the *Mona Lisa,*
and *Venus de Milo* are some of the
many art treasures in the Louvre,
a famous art museum in Paris, France.

The Tower of London is really a group of buildings.

THE JEWEL PRISON

Usually, a prison is a place where criminals are locked up. But there is a prison in London where jewels are locked up. The jewels are the famous "crown jewels" of England. Crown jewels are treasures that belong to a king or queen.

The crown jewels are imprisoned in a place called the Tower of London. The Tower is really more than one tower. It is a group of buildings. One was a fortress, another was a home for royalty, and another was a prison. A high wall and a moat surround the Tower.

Many famous English people heard the dreaded words: "You are sentenced to the Tower!" And some—like Lady Jane Grey, King Edward V, and his brother, the Duke of York—were killed there.

But now the Tower is a showplace where the crown jewels are on display.

In the Tower of London, you can see crowns and rings, scepters and orbs, rods and spurs, and swords and bracelets set with precious stones. Even salt shakers, a foot high and studded with diamonds, are kept in the Tower. The treasures are so valuable that they are guarded by special guards called Yeomen Warders, or Beefeaters.

In one building of the Tower of London, visitors can see the crown jewels of England on display.

THE BELL NO ONE RINGS

Bong! Bong! Bong!

It was July 8, 1776. The tolling of the big bell in the tower of the Pennsylvania State House told the people of Philadelphia that the Declaration of Independence had been adopted. For more than twenty years—since 1753—the bell had called lawmakers to the Assembly and signaled the opening of court. Now the bell was doing what it seems to have been made for— telling the people they were free. For around the upper part of the bell are these words from the Bible: "Proclaim liberty throughout all the land unto all the inhabitants thereof."

At one time during the War for Independence, people feared the British would capture the bell and melt it down to make cannons. So they hid it under a church floor for a year. After the bell was returned to its tower, it was rung every fourth of July. But the Liberty Bell, as it has come to be called, rings no longer. It cracked in 1835, while tolling during the funeral of Chief Justice John Marshall.

Independence Hall (the Old State House) housed the Liberty Bell until 1976, when it was moved to a special place nearby.

The Hall of Mirrors in the Versailles Palace

MIRROR, MIRROR ON THE WALL

Mirror, mirror on the wall
who's the fairest one of all?

If you were walking through the Hall of Mirrors in the Versailles Palace near Paris, France, you would see so many mirrors that you wouldn't know which one to look in first. Almost anywhere you stood, you could see yourself from the front or from the back, from the right side or from the left side.

The Versailles (you say: Ver SIGH) Palace was built many years ago by a French king, Louis XIV. The palace has hundreds of rooms, and it is surrounded by a huge park with fancy gardens and spraying fountains.

The palace is famous for the important things that have happened there: the crowning of the first emperor of Germany, the meeting that started the French Revolution, and the signing of the Treaty of Versailles—the agreement that officially ended World War I.

Now, the Versailles Palace is a national museum of France.

The Versailles Palace and gardens near Paris, France

THE PRICELESS JUNKYARD

What ever happened to the first telephone, the first horseless carriage, the first sewing machine, and the first telegraph instrument? You may think, "Who cares, they would only be junk by now." But you would be wrong. These things may be old, but they are not junk. They are an important part of the history of inventions in the United States.

They have been saved by the Smithsonian Institution in Washington, D.C. They are on display with many other famous "firsts" in some of the buildings of the Smithsonian Institution.

You can see such famous airplanes as the Wright brothers' *Kitty Hawk* and Charles Lindbergh's *Spirit of St. Louis.* You can see Alan Shepard, Jr.'s space capsule, *Freedom 7*, Benjamin Franklin's printing press, and the huge Hope diamond. You can even see the flag that flew over Fort McHenry when Francis Scott Key wrote "The Star-Spangled Banner."

The Italian artist Raphael painted these pictures on plaster walls
in a building in Vatican City, Rome.

PICTURES PAINTED ON WALLS

If your mother wants to decorate the walls of your house, she may
hang wallpaper or she may just hang lots of pictures. But in the
museum in Vatican City, Rome, pictures are painted on the walls
themselves. Such pictures are called "frescoes" from an Italian
word that means fresh. Artists painted the pictures on freshly
plastered walls a long time ago. Many of the pictures show events
from the Bible.

In the Capitol in Washington, D.C., many of the walls and ceilings
are covered with frescoes that show events in the history of the
United States.

This Madonna and Child picture is in the Parma Gallery in Parma, Italy.
It was painted by the Italian artist Correggio.

THE TREASURES OF HORYU-JI

In a beautiful setting of pine trees in a courtyard, stands a group of the oldest wooden buildings in the world. The sun adds a touch of gold to the gray tile roofs.

Atop a five-story pagoda, or tower, is a shape decorated with nine small umbrellas. The umbrellas are a symbol of Buddha, after whom one of the world's great religions was named. The religion is called Buddhism.

This peaceful place in Ikaruga, Japan, is known as Horyu-ji. It's the main temple of a sect, or group, of Buddhists. The group is named for the prince who built the temple more than a thousand years ago. The name of the sect and the prince is Shotoku.

The people of Japan really treasure Horyu-ji. It contains many National Treasures. In Japan, National Treasures include buildings, paintings, sculptures and other art objects. So, besides being the oldest Buddhist temple in Japan, Horyu-ji is also a kind of museum—a treasure house filled with priceless art.

97

Left atrium

Coronary sinus

Left ventricle

EXIT   EXIT

ALL KINDS OF TREASURES

Thump-*thump*, thump-*thump*, thump-*thump*.
You can hear the giant heartbeats
as you walk through a giant model heart.
Inside the heart you can watch the main parts work,
just the way they do in your body.

The giant heart is only one of many treasures
at the Museum of Science and Industry in Chicago.
Another treasure is the Colleen Moore Fairy Castle.
It's furnished with tiny treasures from all over the world.
You can also ride a cage down into a model coal mine.
You can watch chicks hatching at the farm exhibit.
The transportation exhibits include model trains
clicking along on their tracks, old steam locomotives,
and a collection of old-time automobiles.
And in another exhibit, you can
walk through a captured submarine.
You can even inspect the cannons on part of a reproduction
of the gun deck of a famous U. S. Navy warship,
the *Constitution*, better known as "Old Ironsides."

A TREASURE HOUSE OF FOOTBALL

Marching bands blare as football fans cheer the colorful parade. It's 1963 in Canton, Ohio, and football fans really have something to celebrate! It's the opening and dedication of the National Professional Football Hall of Fame. It was here, in Canton, that the American Football Association was organized in 1920. Later, it became the NFL, the National Football League.

Seventeen football heroes are being honored. Bronze busts of these players have been placed in the Hall of Fame. Nearby, life-sized sketches show them punting, passing, running, tackling. Each year since 1963, new members have been elected to the Hall of Fame.

In the Exhibition Rotunda, on the second floor, visitors can watch movies of championship games and other exciting football moments. They can also pick up a phone and hear tape-recorded messages from such memorable players as Jim Thorpe, "Red" Grange, and Byron "Whizzer" White.

The Rotunda also has a collection of trophies, uniforms, and other belongings of famous football players and teams. A library is stacked with books, programs, schedules, and other material about football.

All in all, the National Professional Football Hall of Fame is a real treasure house of football for football fans everywhere.

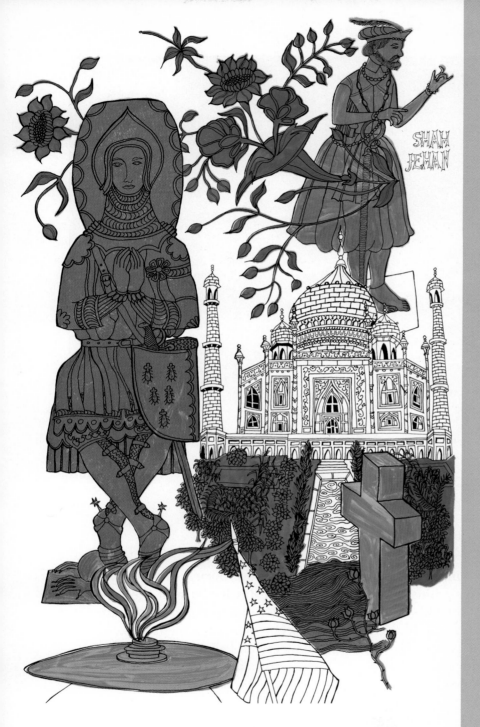

SHAH JEHAN

We may mark graves with a statue, a great monument, a small stone, or with something other than a stone. Some famous people are buried with great pomp and ceremony. Others are buried quietly.

On these next pages, you will learn about places in many parts of the world where you can find all different kinds of famous graves and monuments.

This is the tomb of Richard II and Anne of Bohemia
in Westminster Abbey, London, England.

GRAVES IN A CHURCH

Once, only kings and queens of England were buried in a church known as Westminster Abbey in London. But if you visit the Abbey today, you will see not only the graves of kings and queens, but also of statesmen like Oliver Cromwell, of scientists like Isaac Newton, of poets like Geoffrey Chaucer, and of composers like George Frideric Handel. Some of the graves are so simply marked that you can walk right over them, and not even know it. You might be standing on the grave of Lord Tennyson in the floor, while you are looking at the grave of Chaucer in the wall.

But some graves are large tombs with fancy monuments, and some even have statues of the persons buried there. You can even see statues in memory of famous people, such as Henry Wadsworth Longfellow, who are not buried in the Abbey.

Westminster Abbey has graves in the floors and along the walls.

This early Christian wall painting decorates a tomb
in the catacomb of St. Sebastian in Rome. The flowers
and birds are symbols of happy souls in heaven.

CAVES FOR THE DEAD

Long ago, many people who lived around the Mediterranean Sea
buried their dead in places called catacombs. The best-known
catacombs are the ones the early Christians dug on the outskirts
of Rome, Italy.

Catacombs are made up of tunnels and rooms dug deep in the
earth. The dead were placed in openings in the walls. The graves
were then sealed with bricks or marble slabs. Paintings decorate
many of the walls. Christian catacombs have paintings of olive
branches, doves, fish, and other symbols of Christianity. Jewish
catacombs also have paintings of olive branches and doves, as
well as the seven-branched candlestick, or Menorah, a religious
symbol of the Jewish faith.

For some reason, the catacombs were forgotten for almost a thousand years. They were rediscovered about four hundred years ago.
Today in Rome, you can go down into some of the most famous
of these catacombs.

Empty graves line the walls of the catacombs.
The graves, open now, used to be closed in.

HIDEOUT GRAVEYARDS

Kings of Egypt used to be buried in great tombs
with jewels and golden vases—and even thrones and chariots.
The tombs had so many valuable things in them
that thieves used to break into the tombs
and steal the treasures.
So, later kings decided to hide their tombs.
They left orders for their burials to be
in a secret place called the
Valley of the Kings.
The graves were not to be marked.

But, still, the jewels and golden vases
and the thrones and chariots disappeared.
When historians checked into it, they found out who stole the treasures
—that's right, the men who were supposed to *guard* the tombs.

So if you ever find the grave of a
king of Egypt, you can be almost
certain someone has robbed it before you got there.

Many walls of tombs in the Valley of the Kings in Egypt are decorated with pictures.

Tombs line the side of a hill in the Valley of the Kings near the Nile River.

Tomb of the Unknown Soldier at Arlington, Virginia, in the United States

FOR THOSE WHO AREN'T FAMOUS

Can you imagine famous persons that nobody knows? There are such people. Some of them are called unknown soldiers. Sometimes when a soldier is killed in battle, it is impossible to find out who he was. He has to be buried without a name. So, some countries honor all their unknown soldiers by choosing one and placing him in a tomb for an unknown soldier.

In the United States, the Tomb of the Unknown Soldier is guarded night and day in Arlington National Cemetery.

In France, the Tomb of the Unknown Soldier is not in a cemetery. It is under a famous monument called the Arch of Triumph. An eternal flame burns at the grave.

The English have a different place for their unknown soldier. He is buried in a church called Westminster Abbey near other Englishmen who have been known and honored throughout history.

Tomb of the Unknown Soldier in Westminster Abbey, London, England

Tomb of the Unknown Soldier in Paris, France

Tomb of the Unknown Soldier in Athens, Greece

THE MOST EXPENSIVE GIFT

This old picture shows Shah Jahan, the emperor of India who built the Taj Mahal.

Long ago, an emperor of India built a great tomb in memory of his favorite wife. The tomb was so big and so hard to build that first he had to build a whole town for the twenty thousand men who built the tomb. When the tomb of white marble and red sandstone was finished, twenty years later, it was one of the most striking manmade sights in the world, just as the emperor vowed it would be.

People who visit Agra, India, usually visit the tomb several times. They like to see its gleaming dome. It is especially beautiful in the light of the rising sun and in the light of the moon.

The emperor named the tomb the Taj Mahal for his wife, Mumtaz-i-Mahal. His wife's name means "pride of the palace," and a taj is a crown.

A GIANT BURIAL MOUND

A grave in the city of Sakai, Japan, is so long and so high it looks like a giant's grave. It's about as long as five football fields and as high as a ten-story building! But it's not a giant's grave. It's the final resting place of Emperor Nintoku, who ruled Japan more than a thousand years ago.

It is said that at one time during Nintoku's reign, he saw no smoke rising from his people's stoves. So he did not collect taxes for three years. He also had dikes built to protect the farmlands from flooding. And he had canals built to encourage trading.

Nintoku lived to a very old age. When he died, he was buried in this huge tomb. The top of the mound, shaped like a bell, was covered with cobblestones. More than ten thousand hollow clay figures, filled with dirt, were set along the bottom of the mound. These figures, called *haniwa*, were of animals, people, and all sorts of utensils.

Three moats, or water-filled ditches, surround the giant mound. It's the largest royal tomb in Japan.

BATTLESHIP GRAVE

The battleship *Arizona* sank after Japanese planes
bombed it in Pearl Harbor, Hawaii.

Early on December 7th, in 1941,
hundreds of planes flew over Hawaii
and bombed United States warships in Pearl Harbor.
It was a surprise attack,
and many ships were sunk.
The biggest loss was four battleships—
  the *Arizona,*
  the *California,*
  the *Oklahoma,*
  and the *West Virginia.*

When the *Arizona* went down,
more than a thousand men were trapped inside.
Most of the other ships were repaired and fought again.
But the *Arizona* was left on the bottom,
as a grave for its crew.

Today, a monument spans the water over the *Arizona,*
in memory of all the men who died at Pearl Harbor.

This monument marks the place where the *Arizona* and its crew went down on December 7, 1941.

THE TOMB THAT BECAME A CASTLE

In Rome, Italy, there is a famous castle that used to be a tomb. The Roman emperor, Hadrian, had the tomb built for himself. When he died, he was buried there. Years later, another emperor used Hadrian's tomb as part of the wall built to protect the city of Rome. But the wall was not strong enough. Enemy soldiers stormed and destroyed the city and the tomb.

Legend says that many years later, Saint Michael the archangel

appeared over the ruins of the tomb and saved the people of Rome from a great sickness. So a chapel was built on the ruins. In time, this chapel was enlarged and made into a castle. It was named *Castel Sant' Angelo*—Holy Angel Castle. From the top of the castle, a statue of Saint Michael looks out over the city.

For more than a thousand years the *Castel Sant' Angelo* was the most important fort guarding Rome. Today, it is a national museum. Here you can see a collection of weapons that fills more than fifty rooms. And you can walk up a huge, circular ramp that's part of the original tomb. It crosses over the spot where the Emperor Hadrian was buried more than 1,800 years ago.

WHERE JESUS WAS BURIED

Jesus was nailed to the cross, close to the sepulchre or tomb where He was buried. From this tomb, Christians believe He rose from the dead, three days later.

These holy places are protected and honored under the roof of the Church of the Holy Sepulchre in the Old City of Jerusalem.

In the large church, a carved marble entrance leads to the sepulchre. Made of rock, the floor, ceiling, and walls of the small chamber have been decorated with marble. A marble slab covers the place where the Body of Christ was placed.

Gold and silver lamps burn continuously in the sepulchre. They are kept lighted by members of different Christian faiths who share the church.

In the Chapel of the Angel, a small pedestal marks the place where it is said the angel sat after rolling away the stone from the entrance to Christ's tomb.

If you found a broken tin soldier buried under a big rock, you might try to find out where it came from.

Some grown-ups do almost the same kind of thing. But they try to find answers about how people lived in the past. They find the answers in places like tumbled down palaces, buried cities, and even old statues.

Read the next pages to find out how ruins help unlock some mysteries of people's lives long ago.

The ancient city of Machu Picchu was built by Inca Indians in Peru.

A LOST CITY

They said it couldn't be found. A young American, Hiram Bingham, tried many times and had no luck. And others had tried before him without success.

But Hiram did not give up. He would find one of the lost cities that the Inca Indians had built hundreds of years before, even if he had to climb a hundred mountains.

The Inca Indians ruled in Peru more than four hundred years ago. As one story goes, they built cities near the tops of mountains. Many years later, people kept hearing about the cities, but nobody could find one. Did Inca cities really exist? Hiram thought so, and he was determined to prove it. So he began another climb.

Near the top of the mountain, he saw something through the bushes. Stone buildings, walls, and temples—the ruins of a whole city! He walked in and around the buildings. They were made of huge stone blocks fitted tightly together without any mortar between them. And, instead of streets, steps linked one building to another.

Now Hiram knew that this must be one of the lost Inca cities because it matched the descriptions he had read about them. Nobody knew the name of this Inca city, so Hiram called it Machu Picchu after a nearby mountain peak. Machu Picchu (you say: MAH choo PEEK choo) is an Indian word that means "old peak."

Buildings in Machu Picchu were made of stones that fit together without mortar.

THE GLORY OF ANCIENT GREECE

On a high hill overlooking the city of Athens stand the ruins of a once splendid temple. This famous temple is known as the Parthenon, and the hill is called the Acropolis.

The Acropolis was the religious center of ancient Athens. It was on this hill that the Greeks built the Parthenon almost 2,500 years ago. They put up this magnificent temple to honor Athena Parthenos, the patron goddess of Athens. Inside the temple was a giant gold and ivory statue of Athena.

When Greece became a Christian country, the Parthenon was used as a church. Then the Turks conquered Greece. They turned the Parthenon into a mosque, which is a Moslem place of worship. But during a war, the Turks stored gunpowder in the Parthenon. The gunpowder exploded and the building was wrecked.

Years later, Lord Elgin, an Englishman, visited Athens. He sent home some of the marble sculptures from the outside of the building. Known as the Elgin Marbles, they can be seen in the British Museum in London. Other treasures are in the Acropolis Museum in Athens.

The Parthenon is stripped, wrecked, and worn now. But its ghostly splendor makes you think of the glory of ancient Greece.

THE FORGOTTEN TEMPLE

The big bell-shaped object on top of Borobudur Temple is the main monument.

Trees and twisting vines once completely covered a famous Buddhist temple. It was hidden from sight for hundreds of years. This temple is on the island of Java, which is part of the country of Indonesia. Years ago, workers began to restore the temple. They cut down the trees and vines and dug away dirt. Finally, out of the jungle rose the ruins of beautiful Borobudur.

The temple is shaped like a pyramid with the top cut off. It's built on a hill and has six stone terraces that rise like steps. The temple is so big that if you start at the bottom and walk around each terrace all the way to the top, you will walk three miles (4.8 kilometers). On the top terrace, there is a gigantic, bell-shaped stupa, or domed monument, made of stone. It is surrounded by smaller stupas that also look like giant bells. Stone staircases with carved stone archways connect the terraces. The terraces have blocks of stone with countless carvings that show figures from famous Buddhist books. There are also openings set with statues and more bell-shaped stupas.

Work on the temple continues as other countries help Indonesia with money to make sure the once-forgotten temple will be remembered.

◀ Almost 1,500 stone carvings like these honor Buddha at Borobudur Temple. Buddha's statue sits on the left.

THE GLORY OF ANCIENT ROME

The people of ancient Rome met and mixed at open market places called forums. The most important of these, the *Forum Romanum,* or Roman Forum, became the center of Roman government. The Roman Forum was filled with many beautiful buildings, arches, and temples. There, lawmakers met in the *Curia,* or Senate House. Court was held in the *Basilica Julia.* And public records were kept in a building called the *Tabularium.*

The main street of Rome, the *Via Sacra,* or Sacred Way, crossed the Roman Forum. Victorious generals marched their armies down this street, through the Arch of Septimius Severus, and across the Forum.

After the fall of Rome, the buildings and monuments in the Roman Forum gradually crumbled. In time, people called it the Cow Plain because it looked so deserted. Hundreds of years later, the Italian government began to clear away the rubble. Trees and gardens were planted to make the ruins more attractive. Today, you can see some of the glory that was ancient Rome—including what's left of the Roman Forum.

HIGH-RISE APARTMENTS FOR INDIANS

Two cowboys turned their horses and galloped after a runaway calf that was escaping from a herd of cattle. They found not only the calf but also a deserted building clinging to a cliff. That happened in the late 1800's.

You can see that same cliff house, known as Cliff Palace, in Mesa Verde National Park in Colorado. Scientists say that it was built by the Indians hundreds of years ago. "Mesa Verde" is Spanish for "green table." And that's what the flat-topped hills, or mesas, in the park look like.

The Indians built their cliff house to guard themselves against enemies. It was so big that nearly four hundred Indians lived in it.

No one knows why the Indians moved away from Cliff Palace. Maybe it was because of a war, or lack of rain, or just because they were restless and wanted to move.

These cliff dwellings in Mesa Verde National Park, Colorado, were built long ago by Pueblo Indians.

A church for prisoners and the prison they were jailed in stand among the ruins at Port Arthur, Tasmania.

THE JAIL THAT BECAME A COUNTRY

Strange as it may seem, Australia was first settled because of the Revolutionary War in America. At one time, many countries used their colonies as jails. The British shipped convicts and other prisoners to colonies in America. But after the American Colonies won their freedom, a new place had to be found.

So, almost two hundred years ago, a fleet of ships left Britain, bound for Australia. Aboard the ships were men and women who were being sent away from their country. Some of these people were criminals, but many of them had been put in jail simply because they had no money to pay their debts.

These first Australians settled at what is now Sydney, Australia's largest city. Later, some of the worst criminals were sent to special prisons called penal settlements. One of the main penal settlements was Port Arthur on Van Diemen's Land. This

rugged island, now called Tasmania, lies off the southeastern coast of Australia.

Life at Port Arthur was about as bad as you can imagine. And there wasn't much chance to escape. Guards and dogs kept watch. Shark-filled waters crashed against steep, rocky cliffs. Many prisoners tried to get away, but few ever made it. Port Arthur served as a prison for about 30,000 men over a period of almost fifty years. Then, two years after it was abandoned, most of the settlement was destroyed by fire.

Today, many tourists visit Port Arthur. Among the ruins that have been standing for about a hundred years, you can see the prison and watchtower, a house, a church, and a hospital—all built by the prisoners. The ruins serve as a reminder that Australia is a country that began as a jail.

THEATER OF STONE

All the people in a city can't fit into a theater at the same time to see a movie or a play. Movies and plays are usually shown more than once so that everyone who wants to see them has a place to sit.

But long ago, when plays were first put on in the country that is now Greece, there was only *one* performance of a play.

So the theater had to be large enough to hold all the people who wanted to see the play.

Aristophanes wrote Greek comedies long ago.

Plays by Aristophanes and others were performed in Athens, Greece, at the Theater of Dionysus, which looks like this today.

In the picture, you see one of the first theaters—the Theater of Dionysus, named in honor of one of many gods that people used to worship. The word *theater* comes from a Greek word that means "a place for seeing." The stone seats of the old Greek theater look somewhat like the bleachers of a football stadium.

The Theater of Dionysus in Athens, Greece, is now in ruins. Weeds poke through the seats and stage. But even the ruins of the theater remind us of the days when Greek plays, like those of Sophocles and Aristophanes, were performed there.

PLANTS THAT SWALLOW A CITY

The ancient city of Angkor was discovered about a hundred years ago in the jungle country of Cambodia. Huge stone temples, gates, and walls were choked and covered with vines and tree trunks. Many canals and a hundred pools, some dry, were found around the city.

The only movement was made by bats and beasts. Snakes slithered across the terraces. Who had lived in this spooky place? Who was responsible for building and carving these massive temples?

Little by little, men who studied the ruins of the city have found the answers to most of the mysteries of Angkor. They learned that hundreds of years ago, people called Khmers ruled in and around the land we call Cambodia. The Khmers also built the city of Angkor, which was once the capital city of the Khmer Empire.

Thousands of carvings in the temple walls show barbecued pigs, clawing monkeys, and spear-hurling warriors.

These picture carvings give us an idea about the people who lived in Angkor so long ago.

Recently, people have cleared the jungle from the city with bulldozers. And many of the canals again carry water—canals that once watered the rice fields in the ancient Khmer Empire.

Part of the ancient city of Angkor in Cambodia looks like this now.

A MUSEUM
IN A LAKE

How would you like to visit the kind of village some people in Europe lived in thousands of years ago? You can do just that if you go to the West German fishing village of Unteruhldingen, on the shores of Lake Constance.

Here, on this large lake that borders the countries of Germany, Switzerland, and Austria, you can see a rebuilt prehistoric village. Yes, the village is built *on* the lake, for this is not the usual kind of village. All the houses are on platforms out on the lake. These platforms are built on stilts to raise them above the water. On each platform, there are a few log huts with straw roofs. You get from one group of huts to another by crossing wooden footbridges, also built on stilts.

Houses of this kind are known as lake dwellings. The primitive people who lived here thousands of years ago built their village on the lake to protect themselves against enemies and floods.

This rebuilt village is a museum—the Open Air Museum of German Antiquity. But almost halfway around the world, on the island of New Guinea in the Pacific Ocean, there are people who still live in lake dwellings. Their homes are much like the lake dwellings built thousands of years ago in many parts of Europe.

THE MYSTERY OF STONEHENGE

The huge stones in this picture look like footstools for dinosaurs or building blocks for giants. But whoever heard of dinosaurs or giants living in England?

For years people have tried to solve the mystery of the gloomy group of stones called Stonehenge. Who built it? Where did the stones come from? And why were the stones placed the way they were?

Over the years, some of the heavy stones have tumbled down, but parts of Stonehenge still stand. People visit it because it is one of the few things prehistoric men built that is still standing.

Many scientists have studied Stonehenge. Some say that the prehistoric people who built Stonehenge may have used the stones as a calendar and as a clock thousands of years ago. The stones, they say, are arranged so that they point to where the sun and moon rise and set. If this theory is correct, it shows that prehistoric people were a lot smarter than anyone ever thought.

VEVERS

MME·TUSSAUD'S

THE MAN IN THE IRON CAGE

GLOW WORM

BARON SAMEDI

PAQUETS CONGO

BATS

Any place can be spooky, if it's dark and you are alone. But some places are spookier than others— such places as caves and castles, ghost towns and swamps, waxworks and voodoo islands.

Read the next few pages, and you will find out about some famous spooky places.

STARS OF DEATH

I've never been alone in a dark cave before. I'm glad I have a flashlight.

Look at those huge rock pillars and steeples! I wonder where this path goes?

Oops! It ends at a deep hole! I'd better get out of here.

I think I see some lights up ahead. They look like stars! But how can they be stars when there are walls all around me? Where *am* I?

What I think are stars on the ceiling of the cave are really glowworms. They glisten in a huge, underground chamber in the Waitomo Caves in New Zealand. The eerie lights of the glowworms attract other insects. These insects get tangled in the silky threads that the glowworms spin. Then the glowworms pull in their threads and eat the trapped insects. That's why they're called "stars of death."

Guides lead people part way through the Waitomo Caves on foot. When they reach the glowworm chamber, they get into a boat. As the boat floats slowly through the chamber, they can look up and see "the stars of death." The boat drifts from the chamber to the outside. And it may take them a while to realize that they are outside looking up at the stars in the sky, and not inside the cave looking up at the "stars of death."

The tiny lights in this picture are really glowworms in the Waitomo Caves in New Zealand.

These pictures of a castle in Vianden show one of the many castles in Luxembourg.

THE LAND OF THE HAUNTED CASTLES

Once upon a time, a greedy baron kept a lady his prisoner in the tower of his castle until their wedding day. The lady kept thinking of excuses to delay the wedding, hoping that someone would rescue her. Finally, the lady told the baron that according to a custom of her land, she must weave the cloth for her wedding dress. So, the baron sent a spinning wheel to the tower. But the lady took such a long time with her spinning that the baron became angry. He gave her two days to finish her work. After two days, he asked if her wedding dress was finished. She told him it wasn't her wedding dress, but her burial shroud. Then, she jumped through the tower window to her death.

If you should go to this castle late at night, people say that sometimes you can hear the whir of a spinning wheel coming from the tower.

This is a legend told about the Castle of Ansembourg in Luxembourg. Luxembourg is a little country in Europe which is about the size of the state of Rhode Island in the United States.

In Luxembourg, you can find dozens of "haunted" castles. Stories and legends about greedy barons and knights, hidden treasures, and fairies and ghosts are told and retold by the people of Luxembourg, "The Land of the Haunted Castles."

GHOST TOWN

"Gold!" More than a hundred years ago, this cry sent thousands of people streaming into California. Wild, noisy, gold-mining towns sprang up like mushrooms. One of these towns was Bodie. It lies in a hidden valley, high in the mountains of eastern California. A wandering prospector discovered gold there in 1859.

Soon after the prospector found the gold, he froze to death in a raging blizzard. But word of the gold soon spread and people poured into the hidden valley. The town that sprang up was named for the prospector. His last name was Body. But the spelling was changed. Some say this was because a sign painter misspelled the name. Others claim that the citizens of the town deliberately changed the spelling. It seems they wanted people to call the town BOH dee, not BAH dee.

Over the years, miners dug gold worth millions of dollars from the mines. At the same time, badmen robbed and killed to get their share of the loot. Bodie became known as a wicked town.

Hardly a day passed without some kind of violence. Banks and stagecoaches were robbed. There were bloody fights in the saloons. The streets rang with gunshots and many men were killed.

But when the gold was gone, the people of Bodie packed up and went away. The houses, barns, shops, and saloons were deserted. The hotels, boarding houses, and churches were empty. The schoolhouse, jail, firehouse, post office, and morgue were abandoned. Bodie became a ghost town.

There are many deserted towns scattered throughout the western United States. But Bodie is one of the most famous. It's so famous it's been made a state historic park. If you visit Bodie, you can see all that remains of a town where more than ten thousand people once lived. As you walk down the creaking wooden sidewalk, stop at the morgue. Inside you'll see long wooden boxes. They are coffins—the kind that were used to bury the dead in the nearby cemeteries.

OKEFENOKEE

What kind of place is it
where the earth may shake when you walk on it,
where streams squirm around islands,
where tree roots stick out of the water like bent knees,
where moss hangs like stringy hair from the tree branches,
where alligators bellow, snakes slither, birds screech, bears growl,
and otters may even splash you with water?

The place is Okefenokee Swamp in Georgia
and Florida. The word Okefenokee comes from
an Indian word that means "trembling earth."

At one time, the Seminole Indians camped in
Okefenokee. Hunters and trappers caught and
skinned wild animals there. And people running from the law hid in the swamp.

Now, Okefenokee is a government wildlife
preserve. You cannot hunt or trap there anymore. And you cannot use it as a hideout. But
a guide can take you through Okefenokee in a
flat-bottomed boat, and you can see, hear, and
feel the mystery of a ghostly world.

HOUSE OF WAX

Heads and hands of wax, eyes of glass, real hair, and plaster bodies dressed in real clothes—that's what the "living" statues at Madame Tussaud's waxworks in London, England, are made of. The statues look so alive that sometimes you can't tell the real people from the wax people.

At Madame Tussaud's, you can see statues of presidents and kings, politicians and athletes, writers and churchmen, television stars and movie queens.

And you can go down into a dark dungeon called the Chamber of Horrors and see all kinds of scary things—murderers in the act of committing crimes, a guillotine ready to chop off a head, masks of people made after their deaths, a man strapped to an electric chair, and another sitting in a gas chamber.

After you see the Chamber of Horrors, you can go back upstairs and look for a little, old lady dressed in black with spectacles perched on her nose. When you find her, you will be looking at a wax statue of Madame Tussaud, the woman who founded the famous waxworks.

It is hard to tell the visitors from the statues in Madame Tussaud's waxworks.

The woman in the black dress is a life-size statue of Madame Tussaud.
She is surrounded by statues of famous people.

UNDERGROUND
ROCKS AND ROOMS

Pretend you are riding horseback
along a plain in New Mexico when suddenly
a strange, black cloud whirls up from the ground.
It looks like smoke. But you ride closer, and you see
that it's thousands upon thousands of bats
streaming out of a black hole in the ground.
You light a torch and crawl to the edge of the hole,
but you can't see the bottom.
So, you drop the torch over the edge.
Sparks fly this way and that way as the torch
bounces against the sides of the hole.
Down, down, down goes the torch until
all you see is a pinpoint of light.
This is the way a cowboy, named Jim White,
discovered the Carlsbad Caverns
near the Pecos River in New Mexico.

The underground rocks and rooms are a
fantastic fairyland of shapes that look like
temples and palaces, monsters and pillars,
and dainty, lacy icicles.

The United States government made
Carlsbad Caverns a national park.

LOST IN THE MIST

You are walking on a low, rolling plain. The ground is damp, the air is still, and not a sound can be heard. It starts to rain. Little puffs of mist swirl up from the ground. You walk on. As you trudge along, your feet are getting wet. The rain is getting heavier and the mist is getting thicker. You begin to hear noises like hisses or whines. You walk on. The mist is so thick you can hardly see anything. Suddenly, you think you hear a howl, a scream. Is someone following you? You feel a shiver up your back. You're lost— lost in the mist.

Something like this could happen to you if you were walking on the moors in England or Scotland. Moors are vast, open wastelands. Many mystery writers have used the moors as a setting for their stories. One of the most famous was Sir Arthur Conan Doyle, who wrote the Sherlock Holmes stories.

VOODOO

You are in Haiti—on an island in the Caribbean.
Darkness creeps in and drums begin throbbing.
Voices chant a strange song,
and men and women leap and jump
to the beat, beat, beat of voodoo drums.
A voodoo ceremony is starting.

Voodoo is a name given
to certain religious beliefs and practices of magic.
The people who practice voodoo believe that the
spirits of the dead live in a world of ghosts.
And, they also believe that these spirits come back
to bless or curse the living.

During a voodoo ceremony, people give gifts to the spirits,
and honor them with special songs and dances.
Sometimes, a person will put a hex on his enemy.
Then bad things are supposed to happen to the enemy
until the hex is removed.
Sometimes a wax doll is made to stand for the enemy.
When sharp pins are stuck into the doll, they are supposed
to injure the enemy.

Voodooism comes from West Africa.
When people brought slaves to the West Indies,
the slaves brought voodoo with them.
In Haiti, people still practice voodoo.

THE BLUE GROTTO

To get into the Blue Grotto on the Isle of Capri near Italy, you have to sit in the bottom of a rowboat. And, even then, you have to duck your head when the boat gets to the entrance.

The grotto is a cave carved by the lash of angry ocean waves against the rock. It's called the Blue Grotto because the walls and ceiling of the cave glow with an eerie blue light. The light is a reflection of sunlight on the water outside the grotto.

Is there a place named for an emperor, or a place named by a king?

Is there a place named for some fish, or a place named after some women warriors?

Is there a place named because it seemed peaceful, or are there places named because of their color?

Read the next few pages, and you will find out how some places got their names.

FULL OF BLARNEY

"Aw, you're full of blarney." Maybe somebody has told you that. And maybe he's right. But if you really want to make sure you're full of blarney—according to one legend—you must go to a famous castle in Ireland and kiss a special stone called the Blarney Stone.

That isn't as easy as it sounds.

When you get to the castle, you have to climb up one of its towers. Then you have to lie on your back while you lean out over an opening high in the tower. Two iron bars are all you hang onto while you bend your head backward and downward to get close enough to kiss the stone.

The castle is the Blarney Castle near Cork, Ireland. The legend says that long ago the owner of the castle saved it from attackers by making promises and using flattery. The legend says that the Blarney Stone has a kind of magic power. If you kiss the stone, you're supposed to get the power to become a clever talker. You'll be able to flatter people and talk your way out of trouble. When you do a lot of that kind of talking—whether you kiss the stone or not—people say that you're full of blarney.

This is how you kiss the Blarney Stone.

The Blarney Stone is
in Blarney Castle near Cork, Ireland. ▶

HOW THE LONGEST RIVERS
GOT THEIR NAMES

The falls of the Blue Nile in Africa

The Amazon River, South America

The longest river in the world has more than one part and more than one name—the Nile, the Blue Nile, and the White Nile.

One part of the river, called the Blue Nile, starts at Lake Tana in Ethiopia. The Blue Nile travels so fast that the clay and sand it picks up does not settle to the bottom of the river. So the river is a brownish-blue color. And that's why it's called the Blue Nile.

Another part of the river, called the White Nile, starts near Lake Victoria. The White Nile picks up no sand or clay, so the water is clear. And that's why it's called the White Nile.

The Blue Nile and the White Nile join at Khartoum, Sudan, where their waters become dark blue and continue their journey to the Mediterranean Sea. The word Nile means dark blue.

The second longest river in the world is in South America. It was named after a band of women warriors known as Amazons in a Greek legend. When Spanish explorers discovered this river, they were attacked by a group of Indians wearing headdresses and grass skirts. The Indians reminded the explorers of the women warriors in the legend. So, they named the river the Amazon.

BODY OF A LION— HEAD OF A MAN

What has the body of a lion and the head of a man? No, it's not a monster. It's one of many statues in Egypt that look like monsters. This kind of statue is called a sphinx. The Great Sphinx at Giza, Egypt, is the largest and best known of all these statues. That's why it's called the Great Sphinx.

The Great Sphinx was built almost 5,000 years ago, when Khafre was king of Egypt. Its human head was carved to look like that of the king. The lion body stands for the king's strength. Both the head and body were carved from solid rock. The paws and legs were built of stone blocks. This great statue is 66 feet (20 meters) high and more than 240 feet (70 meters) long. It stands guard over the road that leads to the pyramid built by King Khafre.

The head of the Great Sphinx has been damaged more than once by vandals, people who destroy things on purpose. Over the centuries, desert sandstorms have also worn away some of the stone. Often, the bottom part of the Sphinx lies buried under the sand. But it seems as though nothing can really destroy the Great Sphinx.

163

Brass lions and live peacocks decorated King Solomon's royal palace.

ISLANDS NAMED FOR A KING

Long, long ago, a wise and wealthy king named Solomon ruled in Israel. King Solomon wanted to honor God by building a beautiful temple. The work took several years, but the result was a magnificent building made of white limestone and cedarwood. Gold was used to decorate the carvings of angels, trees, and flowers on the doors. The many tall pillars were inlaid with more gold. At one end of the building stood two large angels, carved of wood. These angels were decorated with more gold. It is said that all this gold was worth billions of dollars.

Hundreds of years later, a Spanish explorer named Álvaro de Mendaña discovered a group of islands in the South Pacific Ocean. He named them the Solomon Islands. Perhaps he wanted his countrymen to think that a great deal of gold could be found on the islands.

Gold has been found on the Solomon Islands, but not enough to compare with the fabulous riches of the Biblical king.

◀ Palm trees rise above a hut on Guadalcanal, largest of Southern (British) Solomon Islands.

CLIMBING MOUNT FUJI

Some people climb mountains just because they're there. Others do it just for the fun or adventure of it. But some people climb Mount Fuji, the highest mountain in Japan, for a completely different reason. These people belong to a sect, or group, in the oldest religion in Japan—Shinto. For them, Mount Fuji is a sacred mountain and climbing it is a holy experience.

Shinto pilgrims wear special clothes to make the climb. They put on a white tunic—a kind of coat—and wear straw sandals. They carry a parasol to protect them from the sun and a staff to help them climb. They also cry out prayers, including a prayer for good weather on the mountain, because the weather on Mount Fuji isn't always good for climbing. In winter, a blanket of snow covers the mountain and makes it harder to climb. That's why many people wait until July and August. Then the snow disappears—except at the very top. Sometimes they also wait until night to avoid the summer sun.

Climbers can rest and eat in stone huts along the trail. The halfway point is known as "the borderline between heaven and earth." At the top of the mountain, there's a large crater you can walk around—for Mount Fuji is a volcano. There doesn't seem to be any danger of an eruption, though. It's been silent for more than 150 years, but sometimes steam comes through cracks in the crater.

To the Japanese, Mount Fuji is known as *Fujiyama* or *Fuji-san*. *Fuji* can mean "fire," "no death," or "never dying." *Yama* and *san* both mean "mountain." But whether it's called Mount Fuji, Fujiyama, or Fuji-san, it's easy to understand why this beautiful mountain is sacred to so many Japanese—especially if you're at the top of it at sunrise.

Istanbul, Turkey

NAMED FOR AN EMPEROR

Many years ago, a Roman emperor named Constantine decided to move the capital of his empire from Rome to a city called Byzantium. Byzantium was in the country we now call Turkey. Constantine made the city bigger and the city was called Constantinople, which means "city of Constantine."

Later, the people of Turkey fought the people of Constantinople and defeated them. The Turks called the city Istanbul. But others still called it Constantinople.

So the city had two names until 1930 when it was officially named Istanbul. "Istanbul" is a Turkish word meaning "to the city."

Istanbul is the largest city in Turkey and one of the oldest cities in the world. You still hear people call it Constantinople, but its real name now is Istanbul.

This old drawing shows how Constantinople looked hundreds of years ago.

WATER, WATER EVERYWHERE

You may know how you got your name. But do you know how some oceans and seas got their names?

The Pacific Ocean was named by an explorer from Spain, Ferdinand Magellan. When Magellan sailed on the ocean, it was peaceful. In Spanish, the word for peaceful is "pacifico"—pacific. But that doesn't mean that the Pacific Ocean is always peaceful. Raging typhoons and tidal waves batter the coastlines of the Pacific many times during the year. Magellan just didn't see any bad storms there, probably.

The Atlantic Ocean got its name from the ancient Romans. In ancient times, people thought that the Atlas Mountains in Africa were the end of the world. And since the ocean was on the other side of the mountains, they named it the Atlantic Ocean.

The Dead Sea in Israel and Jordan got its name from travelers many years ago. They never saw any birds fly over the sea so they thought that the air above the sea was poisonous. But now we know that birds don't fly over the sea because there's no food in it. No fish live in the Dead Sea and only a few plants grow in it because the sea is too salty.

The Red Sea between Africa and Asia could have gotten its name for many reasons. The hills near the sea are a reddish color. So are the coral reefs and seaweed in the sea. And so are the tiny sea animals in the water.

The Black Sea between Europe and Asia got its name because during the winter heavy fogs make the water look dark and murky.

This part of the Cape of Good Hope is called "The Point" in South Africa.

These are fishing boats in a harbor on Cape Cod.

ALL KINDS OF CAPES

A cape can be a coat that you throw over your shoulders. But a cape can also be a piece of land that juts out into a body of water. Some capes were named after the person who discovered them. Others were named because of where they are. But still others were named for fish, fear, hope, and a gray nose.

Cape Cod in Massachusetts got its name because of all the codfish caught off its shores.

Cape Fear in North Carolina got its name because of all the storms in the area. Sailors feared the dangerous waters around the cape.

The Cape of Good Hope at the tip of Africa got its name from a king. When the explorer Bartolomeu Dias discovered the cape, he called it the Cape of Storms. But the king of Portugal hoped that the cape would be a good sea route to India, so he renamed it the Cape of Good Hope. Later another explorer, Vasco da Gàma, proved that the king was right. He sailed around the Cape of Good Hope and continued on to India.

Cape Gris-Nez in France got its name because the cape looks like a big gray nose. "Gris-Nez" means "gray nose."

A SNOWLAND CALLED GREENLAND

When the Norseman, Eric the Red, discovered a large island in the Atlantic Ocean, he thought if he gave it a good name people would want to move there. So he named the island Greenland.

Greenland isn't really a green land at all. It's the largest island in the world, but the only part of the island that's green is the coastline. The rest of the island is covered with ice and snow.

Not many people live in Greenland. Some work as fishermen, some work as farmers, and some work as miners. Others work at weather stations and at an important radar base.

Greenlandic children must dress warmly even in July.

Is there a river that runs backwards?

Is there a place where people grow a plant that is a food and that can also be used to make blankets?

Is there a road that's long enough to reach around the middle of the earth?

On the next few pages, you can learn the answers to these questions and read about some of the other ways we use nature to help us.

WHAT GOOD ARE DIAMONDS?

If you find a blue-gray stone on the beach, it could be more than just a pretty pebble. It could be a diamond.

But you'd have a better chance of finding a diamond in Africa because that's where most diamonds come from. Miners dig for diamonds in blue ground rock. They find this rock underground in or near old volcanoes. Sometimes they have to dig up four carloads of blue ground to find one diamond. That's why diamonds are so valuable—they're hard to find.

You may think of a diamond as something your mother wears in a ring. But some men work with machines and tools that use diamonds. A diamond can cut, grind, and bore holes through tough metals and rocks because it is the hardest substance ever found in nature. Steel workers, miners, and even dentists use tools that have diamonds. You may use a diamond needle to play your phonograph records.

A few of the world's diamonds come from India and South America, but chances are the ones you see or use came from the mines in Africa.

Diamonds are dug out of the earth
and sorted according to size and what they will be used for.

SAVING THE DROWNING LAND

Did you ever hear the story about a little boy whose courage saved his land? His name was Peter, and he lived in a small kingdom known as The Netherlands, or Holland.

One evening, Peter saw water leaking through a hole in a dike. A dike is a wall that keeps water from flooding the land. Peter knew that even the smallest leak in the dike could grow into a flood overnight, so he plunged his arm into the hole to stop the water.

The next morning, the townspeople found him and carried him to his parents. They said, "Give thanks, for your son has saved our land, and God has saved his life!"

You can see many dikes in the western part of Holland. The dikes protect polders—land that water has been drained away from. First, the people build dikes in the water. Then they use windmills or engines to pump the water away from the land. The people can use the drained land, or polders, to grow tulips for people or grass for cows. So you see how important Peter's bravery was.

Windmills help pump water from the land and into canals that flow to the North Sea.

Polders, or drained land, spread across the countryside like a patchwork quilt.

THE BIG ROCK

If you walk around a certain rock in Australia, you really go on a hike—a five-mile (8-kilometer) hike. This great rock is a mile and a half (2.4 kilometers) long and a mile (1.6 kilometers) wide. And if you could climb to its top, you'd be up 1,100 feet (335 meters)—almost as high as the top of the world's tallest building.

From the top of the rock, you'd see flat desert country that makes up so much of Australia. You'd see scattered hills, valleys, and other rock formations. And you'd be standing on one of the biggest rocks in the world. This famous landmark is Ayers Rock, named in honor of Sir Henry Ayers, who was a leader of the government of South Australia.

Thousands of tourists come each year to see this giant rock, which is now part of Ayers Rock—Mount Olga National Park. And Ayers Rock is quite a sight, for it seems to change color in the sunlight. In the morning the rock looks deep purple. But in the light of the setting sun, it is a brilliant orange.

In prehistoric times, Aborigines—the first people to live in Australia—used caves in the rock. The Aborigines painted pictures on the walls of these caves—pictures you can still see today.

STEP FARMING

During a rainstorm, what could happen if you had a hill planted with seeds?

The rain could loosen the dirt and wash it and your seeds down to the bottom of the hill.

Hillside farming is tricky. You have to prepare the hill first, so that the rain won't wash away the dirt and your seeds. One way to prepare the land is to make terraces, like large stairsteps, on the hill. You dig ditches in the terraces and then plant the seeds on the terraces. When it rains, the water will sink into the ground on the terraces instead of washing the dirt and seeds away. The water will help make the plants grow on the terraces.

Many people in Asia live on hilly land. They don't have flat fields, and so they have to use terrace farming. If they want a garden, they have to plant it on terraces, so that their gardens won't wash away.

Many farmers in Asia plant their crops on big flat steps they dig in hillsides.

Peanuts grow underground.

PLENTY OF PEANUTS

How can a cotton farmer earn a living if bugs called *boll weevils* eat all his cotton? A famous scientist named George Washington Carver found an answer. He persuaded some of the farmers around Tuskegee, Alabama, to use their ruined cotton fields to grow peanuts.

The farmers took Dr. Carver's advice. They learned that the ground and warm climate were just right for growing the peanuts.

But Dr. Carver didn't stop his work. He made many experiments with peanuts. He found they could be used for more than just roasting, salting, and eating.

From the peanut, he found ways to make such things as instant coffee, shampoo, salad oil, vinegar, and ink.

Today, Alabama is one of the leading states in producing peanuts. And the farmers have never been sorry that they changed from cotton picking to peanut picking.

◄This statue of George Washington Carver is in the place where Carver worked at Tuskegee Institute in Alabama.

IT'S DONE WITH MIRRORS

When a magnifying glass is held the right distance from a piece of paper, it brings the sun's rays together at one point—the burning point. The heat at this point is so great, it burns the paper.

The sun's energy can also be used to run a solar furnace. Solar means "of the sun," and a solar furnace is one that is powered by the sun. One of the world's largest, most powerful solar furnaces is in Odeillo, France. This furnace is set high in the Pyrenees Mountains, where the air is clear.

How is the sun's energy used to run this furnace? It's used in much the same way a magnifying glass captures the sun's rays to burn a piece of paper. But at Odeillo, it's done with mirrors.

There are 63 large, flat mirrors standing on a hillside. Opposite these flat mirrors is a huge, saucer-shaped mirror that covers one side of a ten-story building. In between the flat mirrors and the big saucer-shaped mirror is a tower with the solar furnace inside.

The flat mirrors on the hillside catch the sun's rays and reflect them onto the huge saucer-shaped mirror. This big mirror reflects the sunlight back to the solar furnace. Steel shutters in front of the furnace control the amount of sunlight that goes into the furnace at the burning point. The heat is so intense at this point it can burn holes through heavy metals.

Right now, this solar furnace is used only for experiments. But someday, solar energy may be used to run factories and heat houses.

TAMING A RIVER

The once-wild Colorado River has been tamed. A mighty dam keeps the river from overflowing and flooding houses and farmlands. Water from the river goes to farms in three states. The river also makes electricity for cities as far away as Los Angeles, California.

The dam that tamed the Colorado River stands in the Black Canyon. Arizona is on one side, Nevada on the other. You can drive from one state to the other on a road that runs on top of the dam. Inside the dam, you can ride an elevator that goes down 44 stories, from the road to a point near the bottom of the dam.

Behind the great wall of the dam, the river backs up to form Lake Mead, one of the largest man-made lakes in the world. At the bottom of the dam, the river water turns giant machines that make electricity.

The dam took thousands of workers five years to build. Before work could begin, the workers had to have a place to live. The workers' construction camp has become the modern town of Boulder City, Nevada.

Tons and tons of material were needed for the dam. A railroad and highway had to be built just to haul supplies to the damsite. Enough concrete was used in the dam to build a highway from New York to San Francisco. And the dam contains enough pipe to reach from New York to Chicago.

This great dam, one of the highest in the world, was called Boulder Dam when it was finished in 1936. It was later renamed Hoover Dam to honor a President of the United States.

These men lived in Starfish House at the bottom of the Red Sea.

LIVE UNDERWATER?

You'd be surprised to look out your window and see a parrot fish, a jellyfish, or a mackerel swim by.

But seeing fish outside his window doesn't surprise an oceanaut. Oceanauts are men who work in the sea. So, of course, they are used to seeing almost all kinds of fish.

Not long ago, some oceanauts from France lived for a month in a steel structure called Starfish House underwater in the Red Sea.

A ship above Starfish House supplied the oceanauts with air, electricity, fresh water, food, and telephone lines. The oceanauts worked underwater several hours a day. They tried to find out more about fish and other things of the sea which people might use someday for food, for clothes, and even for medicine.

In the Starfish House laboratory, the men tested rocks and minerals. And, in the darkroom, they developed films of the pictures they took.

The Starfish House is just the beginning of what can be done underwater. Every year, men explore the oceans and seas in scuba gear, in diving suits, in bathyspheres, and in glass-bottom boats to solve some of the mysteries there.

Today, we get most of our food, clothing, medicine, and building materials from the land. But when you grow up, maybe people will get some of these things from the sea.

This is Starfish House.

Oceanauts explore the area around Starfish House.

HIGHWAY OF ALL THE AMERICAS

With all its roads, the Pan American Highway system is longer than the distance around the middle of the earth. The letters "pan" before a word mean "all." So, "Pan American Highway" means "highway of all the Americas." It links North America, Central America, and South America.

Depending on the direction you're going, the Pan American Highway starts or ends at four different places along the border between the United States and Mexico. Branching off here and there, it goes all the way to Chile and five other countries in South America. But there is still one section of road in Panama that is not finished. People usually put their cars on a ship to go around this unfinished part.

OIL BIRD

COLOSSEUM

KRUGER PARK

Where can you shoot wild animals, but only with a camera? And where can you see a colony of cats? Where is a place where swallows have a schedule? And where is a fortress for Barbary apes? Where do birds fly inside dark caves? And where do dogs save lives in the mountains?

On the next few pages, you will find out where.

"SHOOTING" ANIMALS

Would you go hunting ferocious lions, wild elephants, and fierce rhinoceroses without a gun? That's just what a lot of people do every year when they go on safari in national parks in Africa. Instead of shooting with guns, they "shoot" with cameras.

In these national parks you can see all kinds of animals. These animals are protected by the government. You can ride through the parks and shoot hundreds of pictures of elephants and lions, giraffes and zebras, rhinoceroses and impalas, and leopards and gnus.

If you can't get to Africa this year, you can always practice "shooting" wild animals. Just take your camera to the zoo.

WHERE THE BIRDS COME BACK

People who live in the town of San Juan Capistrano, California,
always know when spring is coming.
The swallows tell them.

Every year the swallows come to San Juan Capistrano
near the first day of spring—around March 19.
The swallows fly to the old Spanish mission of
San Juan Capistrano.
They use the mission as their summer home.

The swallows tell the people of San Juan Capistrano
when winter is coming, too.
Every year the swallows leave the mission around October 23.

No one knows why the birds come and go when they do.
But they always come and go on schedule.
And they always return to Capistrano.

Swallows nest in the
archway of a building
in the courtyard of the
Mission San Juan Capistrano.

This is the courtyard of the Mission San Juan Capistrano.

WE WHO ARE ABOUT TO DIE . . .

Almost 50,000 people roar as fighters called gladiators enter the huge arena. "We who are about to die salute you!" the gladiators shout to the person staging the show.

The gladiators face each other in pairs. They know it's a fight to the death. But if a defeated gladiator really puts up a good fight, the crowd may wave their handkerchiefs. That means they want the man to live.

The Romans loved to go to these combats. In the city of Rome, events like these were held in a place called the Colosseum. This building is about as big as a modern football stadium. At one time, the arena could be flooded to stage fights between ships. Later, cages and dens for wild animals were put in under the arena. The Romans enjoyed fights between animals, and between animals and people. But the most popular of all were fights between the gladiators.

The Colosseum is nearly in ruins now. The gladiators and wild animals are gone. Only tourists and guides—and cats—are left.

MONKEY BUSINESS

What would you do if a band of monkeys stole your dessert? What would you do if monkeys came day after day to steal vegetables from your garden? Such things will probably never happen to you. But they used to happen to people living in a place called Gibraltar.

Gibraltar is a narrow strip of land on the southern coast of Spain. A towering, limestone rock called the Rock of Gibraltar stands at the water's edge. Long ago, the British made Gibraltar a powerful fortress to guard the entrance to the Mediterranean Sea.

Barbary apes, the only wild monkeys living in Europe, used to scamper around Gibraltar. These animals are called apes, but they are really monkeys. A legend says that the apes once warned the British on Gibraltar of a surprise attack planned by the Spanish. The legend also says that as long as there are Barbary apes living there, Gibraltar will belong to the British. So, for good luck, the British keep and protect the apes.

Only now, the apes on Gibraltar can't steal desserts or vegetables. That's because they live in a special place called the Apes' Den.

This is the harbor at Las Palmas, one of the thirteen Canary Islands.

WERE THE CANARY ISLANDS NAMED FOR CANARIES?

You might think that islands swarming with wild canaries and called the Canary Islands were named for those birds. But you would be wrong.

The Canary Islands are near the coast of Morocco, a country in Africa. Long ago, when Spanish explorers landed on one of the islands, they saw large, fierce dogs there. So they named the island "Canaria" which means Isle of Dogs. Canaria comes from the Latin word *canis* which means dog. So the islands get their name because of the dogs, and the wild birds got their name from the islands.

The people of the islands capture wild canaries and train them and sell them to many places in the world for pets.

Another place where canaries are trained and sold is the Harz Mountains in Germany. There, the canaries are trained by "schoolmasters" to sing in a special way.

203

GREAT ST. BERNARD HOSPICE

The towering snow-capped Alps form a giant barrier between many countries in Europe. For thousands of years, the only way to get across the mountains was by means of passes. Travelers faced many dangers, especially in winter. Sudden blizzards might cause them to lose their way. If they lay down to rest, they might freeze to death. Great masses of snow sliding down the mountainside might bury them.

Almost a thousand years ago, Saint Bernard de Menthon built a shelter, or hospice, at the highest point in one of the passes between Switzerland and Italy. The shelter was large enough to care for three hundred people. In time, the shelter became known as Great St. Bernard Hospice and the pass as Great St. Bernard Pass. The monks who lived in the hospice dedicated themselves to helping travelers. To aid them in their life-saving work, the monks bred, raised, and trained the huge dogs that have come to be known as St. Bernards.

The most famous of all these St. Bernards was named Barry. Barry lived more than 150 years ago. He is credited with saving some forty lives. When he died, his skin was stuffed and mounted. Barry can still be seen in a museum in Bern, Switzerland.

But times have changed since Barry lived. Lost hikers and skiers are now rescued by helicopter or by specially trained German Shepherd Dogs. St. Bernards, though, have become a tradition at the Hospice. So the monks still breed and raise some of these dogs. And to this day, the best dog in each litter is named after Barry—in honor of the brave Barry of long ago.

Thousands of people visit the gray stone Great St. Bernard Hospice each year. Many, of course, want to see the world-famous dogs, now bred and raised mainly as show dogs and pets. Even though the dogs are no longer used for rescue work, people still remember the courage of the St. Bernards and what they did so long ago.

Monks at the Great St. Bernard Hospice in the Swiss Alps still raise St. Bernard dogs.

TINY HORSES

A pony is a small, but full-grown, horse. The smallest ponies of all are the ones called Shetland ponies. Many of these tiny horses are less than three feet (90 centimeters) high.

Shetland ponies are named for the islands they first came from—the Shetland Islands, north of Scotland. Even though these shaggy ponies are small, they are quite strong. They've been used as work horses on farms at home and in coal mines in England. In the United States, the intelligent, sure-footed Shetland is popular as a children's pet.

The people of the Shetland Islands also raise small, long-wooled sheep and an unusually small breed of cattle. And to herd their small sheep, cattle, and ponies, they bred small dogs, called Shetland sheepdogs. These dogs look like tiny collies.

A visitor to Kangaroo Island feeds some small kangaroos.

KANGAROO ISLAND

If you want to see a live kangaroo,
the place to go is your local zoo.
That is what most children would do
in most parts of the world—
even in Australia,
where kangaroos run wild and free
in the open country.
But there is only one place in the world
where you can see kangaroos
on an island that is named after them.
The island was named
by Captain Matthew Flinders
who was exploring the Indian Ocean
when he discovered the place
jumping with kangaroos.
That's why he called it Kangaroo Island.

Kangaroos use their hind legs for resting and jumping.

BATTY BIRDS

A cave can be a home for bats and rats, and crayfish and crickets. But some caves are homes for birds. One kind of a bird that lives in caves is the oilbird.

Oilbirds sleep during the day and search for food at night. They are something like bats. They, like bats, have a special kind of radar. They screech, cluck, and squawk. These sounds bounce back to their ears to let them know when things are in their way. That's why the birds can fly in the dark caves or during the night without bumping into things.

If you want to see an oilbird, you can go to the Caripe caves in Venezuela because that's where they live. If you were there, you might learn the word "guacharo." That's what an oilbird is called in Venezuela.

Not everyone can be remembered in a statue. First, you must be famous for something. Kill a giant, ride a horse to victory, or split an apple with an arrow. Then, if people want to remember you, they may pay an artist to make a statue of you.

Sometimes, artists make statues that stand for things such as peace or liberty or other ideas that people want to remember.

The next pages show how some people and ideas became statues, and the places where you can see those statues.

CAPTURING THE SEAS

Once a great English sailor, named Horatio Nelson, helped England become the ruler of the seas. During the Battle of Trafalgar off the coast of Spain, Nelson and his fleet won a fight against the French and Spanish fleets.

It was the greatest naval victory in British history. But Admiral Nelson was killed during the battle.

Today, a huge statue of Admiral Nelson stands on a tall column in the middle of Trafalgar Square in London, England. It is one of the great man-made landmarks of the world. Some people say that if you are looking for a certain Englishman, all you have to do is stand in front of the Nelson monument in Trafalgar Square, and sooner or later the person you are looking for will walk by.

A painting of Horatio Nelson, one of England's greatest admirals

◀ A statue of Admiral Horatio Nelson is on top of the Nelson monument in Trafalgar Square, London, England.

THE GIANT KILLER

Long ago, some people, called the Philistines, had a giant named Goliath in their army. He was so big and fierce that he could frighten almost anyone. But a shepherd boy named David was not afraid of Goliath. When the Philistines attacked David's people, he stepped forward and killed Goliath with just one stone shot from his sling. The frightened Philistines ran away.

When David grew older, he became king of Israel, the land where his people lived.

You can see a large statue of David, as a young man, if you visit the Academy of Fine Arts in Florence, Italy. The statue was made by Michelangelo, an Italian sculptor who lived long ago.

David by Michelangelo
David by Verrocchio ▶

215

STAY ON THE HORSE

Horses have been so important to men that sometimes when a sculptor makes a statue of a person, he includes a horse. This kind of statue is called an equestrian statue. "Equestrian" means "on horseback."

One of the oldest equestrian statues is of the Roman Emperor Marcus Aurelius. It stands near the Capitol in Rome, Italy.

Another equestrian statue you can see is the one of Joan of Arc in the Place du Martroi in Orléans, France. Joan rode a horse when she led the French army to victory.

You can see still another equestrian statue in London, England. It is of Richard I, called the Lion-Hearted, and it stands in front of the Houses of Parliament.

And in Lima, Peru, you can see an equestrian statue of Francisco Pizarro, the Spanish conqueror.

216

Richard the Lion-Hearted ▶

Marcus Aurelius

Joan of Arc

Francisco Pizarro

FROM CANNON AND CONCRETE

Once, the people of Chile and Argentina argued about the border between their countries in South America. Later, they agreed to live in peace and had a statue built to remind them of their agreement.

The Argentine sculptor, Mateo Alonzo, had some of his country's cannons melted, and he used the metal to make a statue of Christ.

The statue was named *Christ of the Andes*. It stands at the top of Uspallata Pass in the Andes Mountains on the border between the two countries. One hand holds a cross, and the other is raised in blessing.

You can see another famous statue of Christ in another country in South America. The statue is made of concrete and reaches as high as twenty tall men standing on each other's shoulders. It has been lighted with floodlights every night ever since it was placed on top of Corcovado Mountain in Rio de Janeiro, Brazil. So, night or day, you can see the statue from the city. You can see the statue even if you're on a ship many miles out at sea. The statue is called *Christ the Redeemer*.

Christ of the Andes ▶

Christ the Redeemer

APPLE AND ARROW

No one can say for sure if William Tell was a real person, but he is a national hero to the people of Switzerland. They tell the story about a time, long ago, when an Austrian named Gessler tried to make the people in Altdorf, Switzerland, bow to a hat on a pole. William Tell refused to bow, so he was arrested. But Gessler said Tell could go free if he could shoot an apple off his son's head with an arrow shot from a crossbow.

Tell shot. *ZING!* His arrow split the apple in half without hurting his son. But Tell had another arrow ready to shoot at Gessler in case anything had happened to his son.

Today, you can see a statue of William Tell in Altdorf. Each summer, actors in Altdorf portray the Swiss hero's life, as it was written by the German playwright, Johann Christoph Friedrich von Schiller. You can see the same three-hour play in New Glarus, Wisconsin, during the Labor Day weekend.

William Tell's statue, Altdorf, Switzerland

THE STATUE OF LIBERTY

One of the largest statues ever made was built in France. It was shipped across the Atlantic Ocean as a gift to the people of the United States. Most people call it the Statue of Liberty, but that's only its nickname. Its real name is *Liberty Enlightening the World*. It is on Liberty Island in New York Harbor. The robed lady stands for liberty, and she holds a torch above her head.

If you visit Liberty Island, you can climb a spiral stairway inside the statue and look out through windows in the crown. At night, special lights in the torch make it look as if it is really burning.

Frédéric Auguste Bartholdi was the man who designed the Statue of Liberty. To make the statue, huge sheets of copper were hammered into shape and put together over an iron framework.

If you visit France, you can see a model of the Statue of Liberty on a bridge over the Seine River in Paris.

A small model of the Statue of Liberty overlooks the Seine River in Paris, France. The original Statue of Liberty overlooks the harbor in New York City.

222

A huge statue in front of Buckingham Palace in London, England, honors Queen Victoria.

QUEEN FOR AN ERA

Whoever the ruler of England may be, one of the places the ruler lives is Buckingham Palace, which is in the middle of London.

In front of the palace, you can see a monument to the queen who ruled England longer than any other ruler. She ruled for most of the century before this one—from 1837 to 1901. And, besides being queen of England, she was queen of Ireland and empress of India.

She was the last English queen to have great power. She did so much to help make England strong that the nineteenth century was named after her—the *Victorian Era*. Her name was Victoria.

The Stone Mountain Memorial on Stone Mountain, Georgia,
looks like this from a distance.

CARVED ON A MOUNTAINSIDE

A giant-sized statue of three men riding horses is carved on the side of Stone Mountain near Atlanta, Georgia. The men were three famous Southern leaders—Jefferson Davis, Robert E. Lee, and "Stonewall" Jackson.

During the Civil War, Jefferson Davis was President of the Confederacy, as the South was then known. Robert E. Lee and "Stonewall" Jackson were the two most important generals in the Confederate Army.

This statue is so huge that once a small crowd of people sat on the shoulder of the figure of General Robert E. Lee.

At first, sculptors used hammers and chisels to carve the enormous statue. Later, they used dynamite to blast the stone so that the statue would be easier and quicker to carve. Then, all work on the statue stopped.

Years later, sculptors began again to carve the statue. This time they used fire to cut into the stone mountainside. Finally, the statue was completed. It took about 50 years from start to finish.

The statue in the center is of General Robert E. Lee riding
his famous horse Traveller. Jefferson Davis is on the left, and
General "Stonewall" Jackson is on the right.

A worker uses a special tool
that shoots fire to carve the statue
of General Robert E. Lee out
of the stone of Stone Mountain.

Abraham Lincoln in Frankfort, Kentucky

Abraham Lincoln in New York City   Abraham Lincoln in Quincy, Illinois

LINCOLN-DOUGLAS DEBATE
QUINCY OCTOBER 13 1858

ABE LINCOLN EVERYWHERE

If you and I drew pictures of an airplane, our airplanes wouldn't look the same at all. That's because no two people draw the same thing in the same way.

That's true with people who make statues, too.

Look at the statues of President Abraham Lincoln, for example. He was such a famous and popular President that many towns and cities in the United States have statues of him.

But different sculptors have had different ideas of how Lincoln looked. So, you hardly ever find two statues of him that look alike. Some statues show Lincoln in crowds such as the one in which he's debating with Stephen A. Douglas in Illinois. Others show him standing in a dignified pose, such as the one at the Capitol in Frankfort, Kentucky. Still others show him as a young railsplitter, such as the statue in Ewa, Hawaii.

But the most well-known statue of the famous President is the one in the Lincoln Memorial in Washington, D.C. There, a huge marble figure of Lincoln sits in a giant marble chair.

Abraham Lincoln in Washington, D.C.

A GIANT AND HIS OX

Many years ago, lumberjacks loved to sit around blazing camp-fires and tell whoppers, or tall tales. And their favorites were stories about the superlumberjack, Paul Bunyan, and his great blue ox, Babe.

There are many different tales about Paul Bunyan and Babe. According to one story, Paul was so big and strong, he could cut down hundreds of trees with just one swing of his mighty ax. And in another tale, it is said that Babe's horns were so wide apart it took a crow forty days and forty nights to fly from the tip of one horn to the tip of the other horn.

In the early 1900's, so much lumber was cut around Bemidji, Minnesota, that Paul Bunyan might have done the job. Now, only one of fourteen sawmills remains. But on the shores of Lake Bemidji, you can see huge statues of Paul and Babe. Babe's eyes light up. They're made of automobile headlights.

BLACK-BEARD

PLYMOUTH ROCK

1620

RAMSES II

Some coastlines are beaches where sand and water meet. But some coastlines have no beaches. Instead, water crashes against the side of a mountain, or water slaps against the side of a glacier. Some parts of coastlines are places where pirates plundered ships, or where noisy sea lions bark, or where tons of whalemeat are hauled ashore.

You can read about many kinds of coastlines on the pages that follow.

Cape Hatteras is sometimes called
the Graveyard of the Atlantic because so many ships
have been wrecked there.

SHIPS BEWARE

You'd run the other way, if you heard that Blackbeard was coming. Blackbeard was a cruel, bloodthirsty pirate from England. His real name was Edward Teach. He had black hair and a long black beard. That's why he came to be known as Blackbeard.

He and his crew used to sail up and down the coasts of the Carolinas and Virginia. They attacked any ship that came into sight. They stole cargo and scared the wits out of the people, especially those who lived along the coasts.

Finally, a governor ordered his men to get Blackbeard dead or alive. Blackbeard was caught off the coast of North Carolina and killed. That same coast in North Carolina, where Blackbeard was killed, is now called Cape Hatteras Recreation Area. The cape has sun, sand, the Atlantic Ocean, and good fishing. That's why people go on vacation there.

Ships that sail along the coast no longer fear the pirate ships. But they still have to be careful. Hundreds of ships have been wrecked in the shallow waters off the tip of Cape Hatteras.

Today, a tall candy-striped lighthouse that was built long ago still stands on the cape. Its light warns ships away from this graveyard of the Atlantic where Blackbeard died.

"THAR SHE BLOWS!"

The city of Sandefjord, Norway, was once an important whaling port. For many years, ships hunting whales sailed forth from Sandefjord to the icy waters of the Antarctic.

High in the crow's nest of a whaling ship, a lookout keeps watch. Suddenly, he sees a foggy mist shooting up from the blowhole on top of a whale's head.

"*Hvalblast!*" he shouts—a Norwegian word that means the same as "Thar she blows!"

The chase to catch the great whale begins! A whaler aims the big harpoon gun and WHING—the harpoon whines through the air. A bomb attached to the harpoon explodes, killing the whale. The hunt is finished.

Over the years, so many whales were killed that some kinds may disappear forever. Today, a group called the International Whaling Commission works to limit the number of whales that can be caught. The group also tries to stop the killing of certain kinds of whales.

So Norwegian whalers don't shout "*Hvalblast!*" as much as they used to, and Sandefjord is no longer a whaling port. But in this city, Norway's great whaling history is recalled by a large stone fountain with bronze figures. The sculpture shows a scene from long ago, when Norwegian whalers rowed whaleboats to capture giant whales with hand harpoons. The full story of those days of whaling glory can be seen in the Whaling Museum at Sandefjord.

Harpoon guns, like the one in this picture, are used to kill whales.
Fountain waters splash about the Whaling Monument at Sandefjord.

These statues and temples would be underwater
if workmen had not moved them to higher ground.

GIANT STATUES ON SHORE

In Egypt, there is a statue so big that eight men can sit on one of its feet. It is one of the giant statues of King Ramses II that stands outside two temples. The temples are called Abu Simbel, built by King Ramses II of Egypt hundreds of years ago. The temples were carved into a cliff along the shore of the Nile River.

When the Egyptians decided to build a new high dam across the Nile, it meant that the river waters rising behind the dam would flood the temples. What could they do to save Abu Simbel and the giant statues?

Egypt, the United States, and many other countries gave money to move Abu Simbel to higher ground. The temples and the statues had to be cut into many huge blocks. Each block was numbered and lifted to the top of the cliff. The numbers helped the workers know how to put the blocks together again. The cliff where the temples were first built is now covered with water.

Before workers moved the stone blocks of Abu Simbel, they put numbers on them. Then they knew how to put them together again in the same order.

Plymouth Rock is under the white roof supported by columns
on the shore of Plymouth Bay, Massachusetts.

Plymouth Rock

THE NOTHING ROCK

If some rocks could talk, what stories you could hear! For instance, one famous rock lay on a barren beach for hundreds of years. Nobody paid any attention to it, not even the birds. It was a nothing.

Then one day a speck appeared far out in the ocean. It grew larger and taller. It drew closer and closer. It was a sailing ship.

When the people on the sailing ship came ashore, they stepped on the face of the nothing rock. If rocks could speak, this rock would have shouted for joy. At last somebody was paying attention to it. The people didn't realize that they were making the rock famous!

That sailing ship was named the *Mayflower*. It brought pilgrims to America from England more than three hundred years ago.

The Pilgrims called the land where they settled Plymouth. Today, people visit Plymouth in Massachusetts to see Plymouth Rock. But they can't step on the rock. It's protected under a stone canopy on the seashore.

Lumahai Beach is on the northern part of Kauai Island in Hawaii.

THE GIANT'S TONGUE

Here's how the story goes:
A mean and grouchy giant once lived on a beach in Hawaii. He frightened people with his bellowing and hollering. He even used to stick out his long tongue at people. But one day a good giant killed the grouchy giant and flung him to the sharks. The sharks ate all of the grouchy giant except his tongue—it was too tough even for their sharp teeth. So they left the tongue of the grouchy giant on the beach where it turned into black rock. Today a long tongue of black rock—all that's left of the grouchy giant—juts into the water along the beach.

Everybody knows that there aren't any giants. But the story of the giant is a story you might hear if you visit Lumahai Beach (you say: LOO mah HAH ee) on the Hawaiian island of Kauai (you say: KOW ah ee).

Hawaii is famous for its many beaches. Perhaps Waikiki Beach in Honolulu is the best known beach of all. But some say that Lumahai Beach in Kauai is the most beautiful beach of all.

241

LAKE IN A CRATER

Crater Lake in Oregon is so big it looks like a bathtub for a giant. The clear, blue water fills the crater of a volcano named Mount Mazama. Scientists say that Mount Mazama exploded thousands of years ago, sending rivers of lava gushing out of its top. Then it was quiet for years, until it finally trembled, cracked, and the edges of the crater fell into the big hole at the top. That's why some people say that Mount Mazama swallowed itself. Water collected in the crater to form Crater Lake.

Today, the lake area in Oregon is known as Crater Lake National Park. Visitors often stay in nearby Rim Village. They can drive their cars on a highway that runs around the rim of the lake.

Sea lions sun themselves on a rocky shore near Florence, Oregon.

KING ON THE COAST

He sits on a rock throne in the center of a cave and barks and bellows and growls. He is the grumpy sea-lion king who rules over the other sea lions.

During the winter months, sea lions gather and live in caves on the Pacific coast near Florence, Oregon.

The sea lions may be fun to watch, but you can't trust them—especially if you're a fisherman. That's because sea lions are so good at stealing fish from fishermen's nets, traps, and lines.

But fishermen aren't the only people who watch the sea lions. Every year, people visit the Oregon coast just to watch the noisy herd of sea lions and their grumpy king.

In the winter, sea lions live in caves such as this one, called Sea-Lion Cave near Florence, Oregon.

The white cliffs of Dover, along the coast of England, are made of chalk.

CLIFFS OF CHALK

Anyone could see that Captain Alfred Bulltop Stormalong's clipper ship couldn't squeeze through the narrow passage of water. "We'll get stuck," shouted the crew.

But old Captain Stormy, as he was sometimes called, did some fast thinking. "All hands grab some soap and lather her sides," Stormy yelled.

The men lathered soap and rubbed the slippery suds onto the sides of the ship. And sure enough, the ship was so slippery that it slid right through the passageway, and it even brushed past some black cliffs along the Dover coast in England. The cliffs scraped off all the soapsuds from the ship, and the suds washed the cliffs white.

That story about the black cliffs turning white is a whopper. But it's still a popular tall tale, especially among sailors.

The passageway of water that the ship supposedly slid through is called the Strait of Dover. The strait separates France from England. On the English side of the strait, lies the town of Dover where the famous white cliffs line the coast. The cliffs are white because they are made of thick layers of chalk. And they never were black.

GIANT BLANKET OF ICE

No sunbathing here! The shore is all ice.

The giant blanket of ice that you see in the picture is the Columbia Glacier in Prince William Sound in Alaska. "Glacier" comes from a French word that means "ice." Glaciers are made when a lot of snow falls on mountains or hills. The snow packs together solidly and freezes and forms a huge hunk of ice.

The sun can't melt a glacier completely because the weather stays too cold.

As the glacier moves, large icebergs break off it and fall into the water—kersplash! But the Columbia Glacier moves so little in one day that even a turtle can travel farther in ten minutes.

This is how the Columbia Glacier looks from an airplane.

You know that a grocery store is a market where you can buy things. But did you know that a street can be a market, a big building can be a market, a city can be a market, and even a boat can be a market?

Read the next few pages, and you will find out about some famous markets.

Most trading in Timbuktu is done during the cooler parts of the day.

A trader leads his camels across the desert to Timbuktu in Mali, Africa.

THE CAMEL AND THE CANOE

If you hear someone say, "from here to Timbuktu," he means faraway. Timbuktu sounds like a made-up name, but there really is such a place.

Timbuktu is a trading center in the country of Mali in western Africa. It's near the south end of the Sahara desert. Timbuktu is sometimes called the meeting point of the camel and the canoe. Every year in the months of March and June, great camel caravans come into Timbuktu. The people in the caravans come from many places to trade goods with one another. Then, when they have traded all they can, they take what's left to the banks of the Niger River. That's when they use canoes. The canoes carry the goods to other parts of Africa.

Timbuktu isn't what it used to be. At one time, it was the chief trading center in western Africa, but now it is more—a military and medical center and a center for Moslem learning.

Piccadilly Circus, London, England

NAMES THAT FOOL YOU

Is there a circus in Piccadilly Circus, or a garden in Covent Garden? Are there petticoats all over Petticoat Lane, or tin pans in Tin Pan Alley?

There is a circus in Piccadilly Circus. But it's not the kind of circus you're thinking of. "Circus" can mean "a round, open area." And Piccadilly Circus is a round, open area that used to be on the outskirts of London, England. Now it is the center of one of London's fashionable shopping areas.

There used to be a garden in Covent Garden. It was part of Westminster Abbey. But now Covent Garden is the chief market place for vegetables, fruits, and flowers in London. It opens early in the morning, and by noon almost everything is sold.

You may be able to buy a petticoat in Petticoat Lane. It is an open-street market where you can buy and see almost any kind of goods. People come from all over the world to buy and sell things. The market is especially crowded on Sunday mornings. Petticoat Lane is really Middlesex Street in London.

There are no tin pans in Tin Pan Alley. Tin Pan Alley is an area in New York City where song publishers have their offices. If you have a song to sell, Tin Pan Alley is the place to try to sell it. At one time, you could hear so many people playing pianos that sounded tinny that people named the area Tin Pan Alley.

Petticoat Lane, London, England ▶

MERCHANDISE IN THE MART

Merchandise is another word for things you can buy, and mart is another word for a place where you can buy those things. Put the two words together, and you have the name of the largest commercial building in the world—the Merchandise Mart in Chicago, Illinois.

The Mart is so big that you'd have to roller-skate around two city blocks just to go around it once. And if there weren't elevators, you'd have to walk up twenty-five flights of stairs to get to the tower in the middle of the building.

Store owners from many parts of the world come to the Merchandise Mart. There they can buy more than a million things to sell in their stores. Most of those things are furniture and decorations for homes.

The Merchandise Mart is also the home of THE WORLD BOOK ENCYCLOPEDIA and CHILDCRAFT, *The How and Why Library.*

Birds are sold on Sundays in the Grand' Place of Brussels, Belgium.

FOOD, FLOWERS, AND BIRDS

You might expect to find a market outdoors where people sell food or flowers. But would you expect to find a market that changes from a food market into a flower market during the week and then becomes a bird market on Sunday? That's the kind of market you'd find in the Grand' Place in Brussels, Belgium. People hustle about buying and selling food during the morning. By afternoon, the food is sold and that's when the Grand' Place turns into a flower market. You can see and smell flowers everywhere in the Grand' Place. And on Sunday mornings, the air fills with the songs of birds. That's right. The Grand' Place becomes a market where you can buy a bird on Sundays.

The Grand' Place became a market place long before the first Pilgrims landed in America. Beautiful gold-trimmed buildings line the market place, and at night, the buildings are flooded with lights that make the Grand' Place look like a golden fairyland.

The Grand' Place in Brussels, Belgium

MEXICAN MARKET DAY

The village square buzzes with excitement. It's market day! People gather from miles around. They have come to buy and sell the products they make and grow.

Sun-ripened fruits and fresh vegetables are spread on the ground. So are dried beans and corn. Some people make and sell clay pottery or cloth. Others sell baskets, brooms, and toys they have made from straw and reeds. And if anyone is hungry, there's sure to be someone making and selling tortillas. These are flat, thin pancakes made of ground corn.

Bargaining is an old custom in Mexico's markets. Buyers and sellers use certain words and gestures that are part of the game. But the first customer of the day always gets what he wants at the price he wants to pay. That's because the seller believes the first sale will bless the day with good luck.

The people of Mexico enjoy bargaining in the market. But this is more than just a time to buy things you need or to sell the things you make and grow. Market day is also a time to see and talk to all your friends.

FRESH FISH!

Your nose tells you when you're getting close to Billingsgate! You smell fresh fish—tons of it—for this is the main fish market of London, England. There you can find almost any kind of fish. Fresh fish is brought in from fishing ports around the coast of Great Britain. The market also imports fish from countries as far away as Japan.

Long ago, the people who worked at Billingsgate used to use some mighty strong language. They cursed and snarled so much that their kind of language came to be known as "billingsgate." Even the term fishwife, which means a woman who sells fish, has come to mean a woman who uses coarse language.

The porters at Billingsgate really use their heads as they work. They wear a special leather hat studded with brass nails. On it they carry boxes with up to 200 pounds (90 kilograms) of fish.

For about three hours every morning, the porters load tons of fish into waiting trucks. Then the trucks speed away to make deliveries of fresh fish to shops throughout London.

A SUIT WHILE YOU WAIT

If your father can't find a suit he likes in the stores, he may have to get one made by a tailor. In most places, it takes a long time to have a suit made. But in Hong Kong your father can have a suit made in a day.

Hong Kong is a busy port on the coast of China. It is not a part of China. It belongs to Great Britain.

Hong Kong is a free port, which means that people do not have to pay a tax on the goods they buy there. Goods from all parts of the world come into Hong Kong to be unloaded and sold, or to be reloaded and shipped somewhere else.

Hong Kong is also a stopping-off point for tourists. They can ride in jinrikishas, buy cakes that are sold from rowboats, have suits made in one day, or buy food at night markets.

Wall Street in New York City has tall buildings that rise like walls. The building with the tower is Trinity Church.

Members of the New York Stock Exchange buy and sell stocks there.

WHERE STREETS ARE MARKETS

In New York City, some street names have special "meanings."

Fifth Avenue means EXPENSIVE CLOTHES.
On Fifth Avenue, you can buy all kinds of expensive clothes in store after store. Many of the stores sell only original clothes, which means the clothes are the only ones of their kind. So if you're looking for expensive clothes in New York City, you go to Fifth Avenue.

Broadway means THEATER.
You can see the best plays and shows on Broadway. But a strange fact is that most Broadway theaters are not actually on Broadway. They are on streets that lead into Broadway.

Madison Avenue means ADVERTISING.
Most of the advertising agencies in New York City are on Madison Avenue. If you want to buy some advertising or if you know how to sell advertising, Madison Avenue is the street you want.

Wall Street means STOCK MARKET.
One of the biggest stock markets in the world is on Wall Street. There you can buy and sell stocks and bonds of businesses from all over the world.

The theater district of Broadway in New York City is known as the "Great White Way" because of the many lights.

FLOATING MARKETS

If you go shopping in Bangkok, Thailand, you don't have to shop in a store, you can shop on a boat. The boats are called sampans. And they float on the Chao Phraya River, which flows through the city of Bangkok.

The merchants sell salt, rice, charcoal, medicines, coconuts, clothing, and souvenirs.

These floating markets of Bangkok do double duty. After a merchant sells his goods, you might see him using his sampan to deliver mail to homes or to take children to school.

Floating markets got started in Bangkok because long ago there were only a few roads. People had to travel by boat.

Even though Bangkok now has roads, many people of Thailand still shop at floating markets.

CHEESE FOR SALE!

If you like cheese, you'd love Alkmaar. It's the most famous cheese market in The Netherlands. Truckloads of cheese arrive in Alkmaar early Friday morning. The trucks come from around the city of Edam. That's where the cheese is made, which is why it's called Edam cheese.

In the clock tower of the Weigh House, a wooden trumpeter raises his horn and horsemen appear. They thrust out their swords each time the clock strikes. After ten thrusts, they disappear. It's ten o'clock, time for the cheese sale to begin.

Merchants test the cheese and farmers quote prices. When a sale is made, the porters take over. Their white suits and colorful straw hats flash in the sun as they pack the cheese on large, rocker-shaped barrows. The colored hats and barrows show which company the porters work for. The porters work in pairs. They load up to eighty rounds of cheese on a barrow. Then they hook their harnesses to the barrow and run to the Weigh House. After being weighed, the cheese is sent on its way. You'll find Edam cheese at the grocery store. It's good!

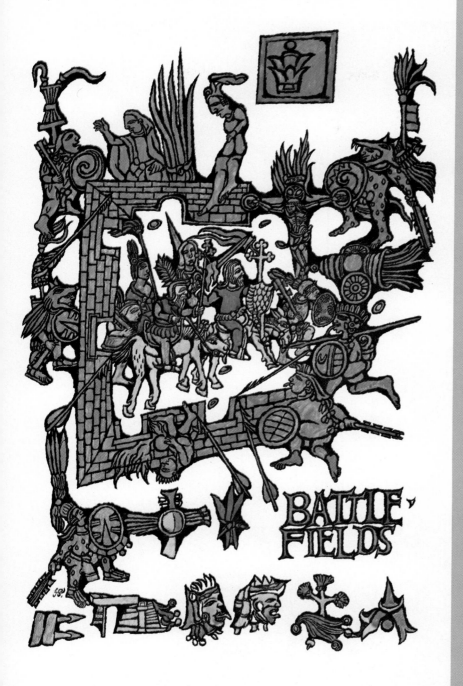

BATTLE FIELDS

Men have battled in cities, at fortresses, in the open countryside, and on the seas. Sometimes the battles are so important that the battlegrounds become famous.

On the next pages, you will visit some of the most famous battlegrounds in the world.

Thousands of Mexican soldiers fought against Texas soldiers in the Alamo years ago.

REMEMBER THE ALAMO

"Victory or death—I shall never surrender or retreat." Those were the words of Colonel Travis who defended the Alamo with about one hundred fifty soldiers of the Texas Army.

The colonel and his men were trapped inside a mission, called the Alamo, that they were using as a fort. Santa Anna, the Mexican leader, waited outside the Alamo with more than a thousand soldiers. He knew that the Texans did not have many supplies. Colonel Travis sent messengers for help, but no help came. Still he would not give up. Finally, Santa Anna ordered his men to charge. They killed every soldier in the Alamo. Men such as Davy Crockett and Jim Bowie fought so bravely that even their enemies told stories of their courage. "Remember the Alamo" became a cry that inspired soldiers in other battles.

Today, you can visit the Alamo in San Antonio, Texas, and see the mission that turned into a battleground. It is a peaceful place with a museum full of things from the past, a library full of books, and gardens full of flowers.

The Alamo is the place where Davy Crockett and Jim Bowie died defending Texas.

D-DAY BEACHES

When is D-day? That's a military secret because a D-day is a day when an invasion begins. During World War II, D-day was supposed to be June 5, 1944. Almost three million men from the armies of the United States and its allies were all set to invade the beaches of Normandy and drive Adolf Hitler's army out of France. But the weather was stormy, so the leader of the invasion, General Eisenhower, commanded the armies to wait. In the early morning of June 6, gliders landed in enemy territory, ships fired their big guns, airplanes dropped bombs, and the Allies landed on the beaches. It was the most famous D-day of all—the beginning of the end of World War II.

Today, the quiet Normandy beaches are still strewn with reminders of the invasion on D-day.

This landing on Normandy Beach on June 6, 1944, was the beginning of the Allied march across France.

Today, German fortifications that couldn't stop the ▶ Allied landing still stand on Normandy Beach.

THE RED BRICK WALL

Long ago, some African people, called the Moors, built a fortress in Granada, Spain. They also built a palace behind the red brick walls of the fortress. They called the fortress and palace "Alhambra," an Arabic word that means "the red."

In 1492, the same year that Columbus sailed for America, King Ferdinand and Queen Isabella of Spain ordered their armies to attack the Moors. The Spanish Army marched to the Alhambra at the foot of the Mulhacén, the highest mountain in Spain. The Moors lost the battle and the Alhambra, which was their last stronghold in Spain.

Through the years, the Alhambra began to crumble. No one did much to preserve it until after the American writer Washington Irving went to live in Spain for a while.

Irving wrote a book called *The Alhambra*. His book stirred people to save the Alhambra from becoming a ruin. Today, you can walk through the gardens of the Alhambra and look up at the steep mountains.

◀ The Alhambra in Granada, Spain

The Court of the Lions has a fountain surrounded by stone lions.

Citizens of France freed prisoners from the Bastille in Paris during the French Revolution.

FREE FOR ALL

"Storm the Bastille! Free the prisoners!"

That's what an angry crowd shouted as they ran through the streets of Paris, France, on July 14, 1789.

The French Revolution had already begun. And the people wanted to free the prisoners jailed in the Bastille to show King Louis XVI how much they hated the way he treated all Frenchmen.

When Governor De Launay lowered the drawbridge of the Bastille to let in some of the king's troops, the crowd rushed inside, too. They killed the guards and freed the prisoners. The next day they began to tear down the Bastille, and today only a few stones remain.

Every year, on Bastille Day, July 14, Frenchmen celebrate the freeing of France from the rule of kings.

CUSTER'S LAST STAND

General Custer fought many Indian battles. So, when he and his men received orders to help round up the Sioux and the Cheyenne Indians, Custer thought the job would be easy. He had six hundred fifty men and figured there'd be about one thousand Indians in a village near the Little Bighorn River in what is now Montana.

Custer divided his men into three groups and ordered them to attack. Custer's group went around to the right of the village, planning to surprise the Indians from behind. Instead, the Indians surprised them—thousands of angry Indian warriors. They slaughtered Custer and all the men of his group. Only a horse survived.

Today, you can see the Custer Battlefield, a national monument, in Montana. You can see the marble slabs that mark the places where Custer and his men fell.

This painting by Frederic Remington is called *Custer's Last Stand*.

The Custer Battlefield National Monument in Montana has many stone markers on places where Custer's men died.

IT SOMETIMES PAYS TO BE SMALL

More than three hundred years ago, the small English Navy met
and defeated the big Spanish Armada in the English Channel.

Long ago, when most boats had sails, the people of Spain called
their navy the Invincible Armada. Invincible means unbeatable,
and an armada is a fleet of warships. When King Philip II of Spain
ordered the Armada to attack England, the people of Spain
cheered as the ships sailed out of the harbor. They thought their
ships would win the war for sure. Many of the Spanish ships were
like floating fortresses. Most of the ships of the English Navy were
small, and some of them weren't even warships.

The sailors on the Spanish and English ships started to fight in the
English Channel. The English sailors would fire a shot, get out of
range, and come back to fire again. After days of battle, the little
English ships beat the Invincible Armada. From that battle on,
for many, many years, England controlled the seas.

"FOUR SCORE AND SEVEN YEARS AGO"

In Gettysburg, Pennsylvania, you can see the place where one of the bloodiest battles of American history was fought. Some people say that the Battle of Gettysburg was the turning point in the Civil War. General George G. Meade and his Northern troops met General Robert E. Lee and his Southern troops at Gettysburg. General Lee lost the battle after three days. So many men were killed that people came from many parts of the country to look for dead relatives on the battlefield. Today almost one thousand unknown soldiers are buried in a graveyard there. President Lincoln dedicated the cemetery with one of his most famous speeches—the Gettysburg Address. It began "Four score and seven years ago. . . ."

In Gettysburg, you can see statues of General Meade and General Lee as well as the graves of the thousand unknown soldiers. And the large Soldiers' National Monument stands on the spot where Lincoln made his famous speech.

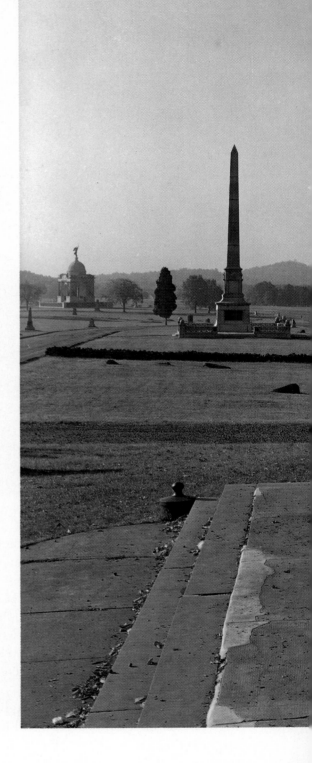

This cemetery is called Gettysburg Military Park.
It is where the Battle of Gettysburg was fought.

THE TREE OF THE SAD NIGHT

This drawing shows the army of Hernando Cortes fighting the Aztec Indians long ago.

The Tree of the Sad Night in Tacuba, Mexico

Long ago, Hernando Cortes of Spain decided to capture the Aztec Indian city of Tenochtitlán in what is now Mexico. The Aztec leader, Montezuma II, thought Cortes was an Aztec god named Quetzalcoatl. Montezuma welcomed Cortes and his army into the city with gifts of gold. The Aztec had never seen guns and horses. And Cortes had never seen anything like Tenochtitlán with its palaces, pyramids, and floating gardens. He wrote to his king that it was the most beautiful city in the world.

The Aztec became angry with both Cortes and Montezuma. One night they killed many of Cortes' men and drove Cortes out of their city. It is said that after the battle Cortes sat under a tree and wept. The night is remembered as "La Noche Triste," which means "The Sad Night."

And today in a place called Tacuba, near Mexico City, you can still see the Tree of La Noche Triste—the tree Cortes sat under.

After the battle of La Noche Triste, Cortes came back and conquered the city of Tenochtitlán—the city we call Mexico City.

THE FORTRESS THAT DIDN'T WORK

You'd have to travel 100 miles (160 kilometers) an hour for two whole hours to get from one end to the other of a line of fortresses along the eastern border of France. And you'd have to pay two million dollars a day every day from January through most of July to build this long line of fortresses.

It's called the Maginot Line, and it got its name from André Maginot, a French hero of World War I. The Maginot Line was built after World War I and before World War II to protect France from Germany.

Along the Maginot Line, French soldiers rode elevators down to their living quarters underground. They raced on bicycles with messages through the tunnels between the forts. Others carried supplies on a special underground railroad.

Today, much of the underground parts of the Maginot Line have been made into bomb shelters. The Royal Canadian Air Force stores supplies in another part of it. And one of the forts is a radar station.

You'd think such a fort would really protect France. But during World War II, the Maginot Line didn't help France a bit. The Germans just went around it.

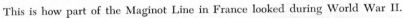
This is how part of the Maginot Line in France looked during World War II.

When you have a favorite toy that breaks, you fix it and make it almost as good as new.

Buildings and castles and cities don't break. But sometimes they wear out and need fixing, too.

When we make a building or a castle or a city look the way it did when it was first built, we call it a restoration.

Read the next few pages, and you will find out about some famous restorations.

The Raleigh Tavern in Williamsburg, Virginia, has been made to look just as it did in colonial days. The people are dressed in colonial costumes.

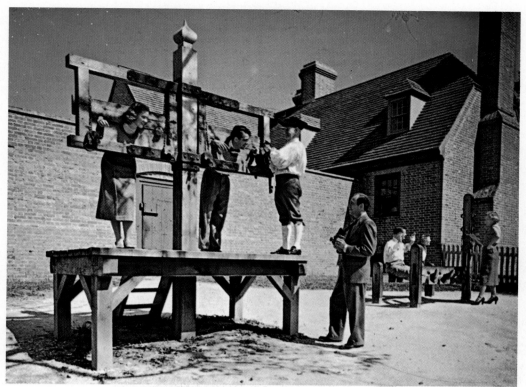

Visitors to Williamsburg, Virginia, can be placed in pillories and stocks just for fun.

PILLORY AND STOCKS

Long ago, many troublemakers in colonial America were punished in public. They were locked in wooden frameworks in the town square, where everyone could see them.

One of these frameworks, called a pillory, had holes for the head and hands. If you were locked in it, you couldn't dodge the things people might throw at you. Another framework was the stocks. It had holes in which the troublemaker's ankles were locked. But at least he could sit down. Sometimes troublemakers were whipped at whipping posts. People aren't punished like this anymore. But in Williamsburg, Virginia, you can see a pillory, the stocks, and a whipping post.

Williamsburg was once the capital of the Virginia Colony. Many of the buildings have been rebuilt, and today this historic city looks much as it once did. The people who work there even dress in the kinds of clothes worn long ago. A visit to Williamsburg is like a visit to yesterday.

◀ This man is showing how a bootmaker worked in colonial days.

The Pantheon in Rome, Italy, was built
thousands of years ago and looks like this today.

A ROOF WITH A HOLE
IN THE MIDDLE

Whoever heard of building a building with a big hole in the
middle of the roof? No, the hole was not a mistake; it was put
there on purpose.

The building with a big hole in the middle of the roof is the
Pantheon in Rome, Italy. It has no windows or lamps. Light comes
through the big hole in the roof.

Long, long ago, a Roman general named Marcus Agrippa built
the Pantheon as a temple to honor all the Roman gods. Later, the
Emperor Hadrian added the big round dome-area, called the
rotunda. The rotunda measures about fourteen stories from floor
to ceiling and from side to side. And the huge dome with the big
hole in the middle is one of the biggest domes in the world.

You can see the Pantheon in the Piazza della Rotunda in Rome. It
is one of the best-preserved examples of ancient Roman archi-
tecture in the world.

This old painting shows how the hole in the roof
of the Pantheon helped to light the inside of the building. ▶

WHAT A CASTLE REALLY WAS LIKE

All kinds of kings and all kinds of lords built all kinds of castles in Europe long before the United States became a country.

Many castles are no more. Others have fallen apart and stand in ruins. But Bunratty Castle near Shannon Airport in County Clare, Ireland, has been rebuilt. It looks the way it did when it was first built. We call it a restoration.

Restoring a castle takes a lot of time and money. A man named Lord Gort restored the castle inside and out with the help of the Irish government. Workers replaced bricks and stones, cleaned walls and floors, and found furniture and paintings like the ones used in the castle when it was first built.

Bunratty Castle is now an Irish national monument. Many tourists visit it to see what a castle really was like a long time ago.

At Bunratty Castle in Ireland, people dress in costumes and serve meals as they did long ago.

The *Constitution,* a famous sailing ship, looks like this today.

A SHIP SAVED BY A POEM

"Oh, better that her shattered hulk
Should sink beneath the wave;
Her thunder shook the mighty deep,
And there should be her grave;"

This is part of a famous poem written by a famous American writer, Oliver Wendell Holmes. The poem is "Old Ironsides," and it saved a famous ship, the *Constitution,* from being junked.

The *Constitution* was a sailing ship with three masts. It was used by the United States Navy in the 1800's. It got its nickname "Old Ironsides" during a battle with an English warship during the War of 1812. Shots from British guns seemed to bounce off the sides of the *Constitution* as though the ship had sides made of iron.

After many battles, the government decided that the ship was no longer seaworthy and wanted to destroy it. Then Oliver Wendell Holmes wrote his famous poem. The people of the United States became aroused and didn't want the ship destroyed. So the government rebuilt it and restored it.

Thousands of people visit the *Constitution* every year in the Boston Navy Yard.

This painting shows how the *Constitution* looked when the ship was in full sail.

LET THERE
BE PEACE

Peace Memorial Park is the only park of its kind in the world. This park is in the center of the city of Hiroshima, Japan. It marks the spot where the first atomic bomb was dropped.

During World War II, Hiroshima was an important Japanese military base. On the morning of August 6, 1945, three American planes appeared over the city. One of them dropped a single atomic bomb that destroyed most of the city. Three days later, a second atomic bomb was dropped on Nagasaki. And on September 2, the war officially ended.

Hiroshima is now a busy, modern city. It's been rebuilt by the courageous Japanese people. But there are reminders of the terrible tragedy of the atomic bombing. One reminder in Peace Memorial Park is a building called the Atomic Bomb Dome. The building stands on the banks of the Ota River, as it did before the atomic bomb fell. But now it stands in ruins. It was left there to remind everyone of the horrors of atomic war.

Peace Memorial Park also has a special monument that contains a stone chest with the names of those killed in the first atomic bombing.

Children of different Indian tribes do a war dance
in front of a Wichita grass house in Indian City, Oklahoma.

A CITY OF WIGWAMS

You can see Kiowa tepees, Apache wickiups, Wichita grass houses, Comanche settlements, Caddo lodges, and Pawnee earth villages in Indian City, U.S.A.

Indian City is in the Tonkawa Hills near Anadarko in Oklahoma. The people of Anadarko built the city with the help of Indians. Everything in the city is Indian—the houses, tools, furniture, art, weapons, musical instruments, and clothing.

Indian guides take you through the city and explain the customs of the different tribes. You can even see real Indian dances at Indian City, U.S.A.

This kind of Indian hut is called an Apache wickiup.

THE TOWN THAT SILVER HELPED BUILD

If you climb a certain hill in the middle of Mexico, you will find a town that silver helped build. The town is Taxco (You say: TAHS koh).

Silver from the rich mines of Taxco helped pay for the red-tiled roofs, the cobblestone streets, and one of the most colorful churches in Mexico—Santa Prisca. The church has an altar set with gold. The towers of the church are rose-colored and rise high above the rows of little white houses.

Once, the silver mines of Taxco were so rich that a Spanish soldier named Cortes used the silver to make silver cannons. Those cannons helped him to conquer Mexico.

But the mines finally had no more silver, and today Taxco is just a quiet little town. Artists go to Taxco to paint, and tourists buy silver trinkets or watch the fireworks at fiesta-time.

The government of Mexico has made Taxco a national monument to make sure that the town will always look the way it looks today.

Taxco, Mexico

George Washington's card table

George Washington's desk

Martha Washington's dressing room

GEORGE WASHINGTON SLEPT HERE

Sometimes a building becomes famous because an important person slept there. Many times we don't know that the person really did stay there. But we can be sure there is at least one place where George Washington slept. It was his home—Mount Vernon.

Mount Vernon is in Virginia near Washington, D.C. Its mansion looks the same way it did when George Washington lived there. You can see the bed that he slept in, the desk where he wrote, the harpsichord that he played, a telescope that he used, and many of the books that he read.

You can also see the tomb of George Washington and his wife Martha on the grounds at Mount Vernon.

◀ The kitchen in Washington's home
in Mount Vernon, Virginia

STREET OF STEPS

Part of the modern city of San Juan, Puerto Rico, is Old San Juan. Here, the government has rebuilt and restored many old buildings and streets. Now, tourists and others can see what Old San Juan looked like, long ago.

One old street is unlike any other. It has wide steps that lead from one landing to another. It is a street for people, not cars. It was built this way so that it would be easy for people to walk up the hill.

This street of steps was named for nuns who once lived in a convent there. The nuns moved away, and the convent later became a modern hotel. But the street is still called "Callejón de las Monjas," Spanish for "Street of the Nuns."

"Street of the Nuns" is a street of steps in Old San Juan, Puerto Rico.

PULLED OUT OF A SLUM

When Jane Addams turned Hull House in Chicago into a settlement house, it was because of a slum. She wanted a place where the poor people of the neighborhood could come for help. So she rented an old building that once had been the home of a Chicago pioneer, Charles J. Hull. Soon, the lady who owned Hull House gave it to Jane Addams.

As time went on, Hull House grew into many buildings. But now the only one that remains is the original building. This building has been restored as a memorial to Jane Addams and to all the good work she did to help people. The building is located on the University of Illinois campus in Chicago, Illinois.

Hull House, Chicago, Illinois

What happens when you want to get to the other side of a mountain, when you can't climb it? How do you get to the other side of a lake or a river, when you don't have a boat? How do you get a boat from one body of water to another, when there's land in between?

Read the next few pages, and you will find out what people in different parts of the world do when nature gets in the way.

George Donner led a group of pioneers through this mountain pass to California.
The Donner Pass was named after him.

DONNER PASS

"California or Bust!" That's what some of the early pioneers shouted as they traveled westward in wagon trains. The pioneers had to find a pass through a range of mountains called the Sierra Nevada in order to reach California. They found the pass and many crossed the mountains with few hardships. But one group—the Donner Party—was not so fortunate.

The Donner Party reached the mountains just as a snowstorm started. It snowed so much that they could not get their wagons through the mountain pass. So they camped there. When the snow stopped, they tried again, but they could not make it. The pioneers did not have much food, but they had some cattle. And between snowstorms, they thought they could hunt. The cattle wandered away and froze in the snow, and there were no animals to hunt. So they killed many pets for food. Every day small groups tried to make it over the pass, but they had to turn back. Finally, one group made it to California. They sent back rescue parties with supplies.

Many people in the Donner Party died that winter trying to cross the mountain pass. The pass was named Donner Pass in their honor.

Years later, the first transcontinental railroad crossed the Sierra Nevada through the Donner Pass. And now a highway runs along the pioneer trail.

Today, people can travel through Donner Pass on the Donner Pass Highway.

CITY OF CANALS

In Venice, Italy, the streets are canals. So instead of seeing cars, you can see flat-bottomed boats called gondolas.

Venice is built on a cluster of small mud islands. The canals twist around the islands. The biggest canal, called the Grand Canal, winds through the center of the city and separates the islands into two main groups.

People didn't have to build the Grand Canal. It was already there. But they did have to find a way over it. So they built beautiful bridges across the Grand Canal. These bridges connect the island groups. Houses, palaces, and churches line the canal. And posts that look like giant peppermint sticks are used to keep gondolas from floating away when they're not in use.

At one time, Venice was a major Italian trading port. Now, much of the trade goes to other ports. But Venice is still famous for its beauty and romance, its canals and gondolas.

People in Venice, Italy, travel through canals in boats called gondolas.

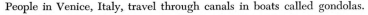

This is how Old London
Bridge looked long ago.

This is how the granite
London Bridge looked.

LONDON BRIDGE IS FALLING DOWN

"London Bridge is falling down,
Falling down, falling down,
London Bridge is falling down, my fair lady."

The London Bridge that was forever "falling down" in the nursery rhyme was built of stone. It was built across the River Thames in London and lasted for more than 600 years.

During those years, the bridge suffered many accidents. Ships crashed into it. The weight of traffic made it crack and sink a little. The pounding river loosened it. And it had to be repaired again and again. Some of the money for the repairs came from rent paid by people with shops on the bridge. The repairs cost so much that the people of London decided to tear it down and build another London Bridge of a strong rock called *granite*. But in time, it, too, began to crack and sink a little. So again, the people decided to take down that bridge and build a new London Bridge made of concrete.

The granite bridge was taken apart piece by piece and shipped to the United States to be put back together again across an artificial lake in Arizona.

This is an artist's drawing of London Bridge at its new Arizona home in the United States.

Trains travel between Italy and France through the Mont Cenis Tunnel.

HOW TO MAKE A TUNNEL

You can dig a little tunnel with your hands, or with a spoon, or with a shovel. But how would you dig a tunnel through a mountain?

The Mont Cenis Tunnel is a railroad tunnel through the Alps. It connects France and Italy. It was the first tunnel ever built through the Alps. People could not get over the Alps by railroad, so the governments of France and Italy decided to build a tunnel.

Two groups of men worked on the tunnel. One group started working in France. The other group started working in Italy. For the first time, men used a new drill called a power drill. They used it to make small holes in the mountain. The men filled the small holes with gunpowder and lit a fuse. The gunpowder blasted big holes in the mountain. Then the men dug out the rocks and started to drill again.

It took as long as it takes a baby to grow into a teen-ager for the workers from France and Italy to meet. But when they did, the first tunnel through the Alps was finished.

Now people can travel by train from France to Italy and from Italy to France through the Mont Cenis Tunnel.

Workers of France and Italy finished building the Mont Cenis Tunnel in 1870.

BY CAMEL, BY CAR, BY TRAIN

There's a special road for camels, and a special road for cars, and a special road for trains, and they all go through the Khyber Pass in West Pakistan.

The Khyber Pass connects Pakistan and Afghanistan. The pass is the lowest place between two huge mountain ranges. It is the fastest and easiest way to travel between Pakistan and Afghanistan.

Small tribal villages lie on both sides of the pass. The villages are walled and have watchtowers, because the people in the different villages are always quarreling and fighting. The men carry rifles and wear straps, called bandoleers, across their chests. The bandoleers have places for bullets. The Khyber Pass is dangerous because of the tribal wars and the bandits who rob travelers.

Warning signs in different languages are at the entrance to the Khyber Pass.

Roads such as these zig-zag through the Khyber Pass.

A ship enters the locks of the Panama Canal.

Gates in the locks of the Panama Canal
open to let the ship through.

WHERE OCEANS MEET

What's the shortest sea route between New York City and San Francisco? Through the Panama Canal!

Before the canal was built, ships had to sail all the way around South America to travel between those cities. So, the United States government built the canal through the Isthmus of Panama in Central America. The canal connects the Atlantic Ocean and the Pacific Ocean.

A ship sailing from the Atlantic Ocean enters the canal through a bay. The ship sails through the bay and through a channel into a set of locks. Then water is let into the locks, and the ship is lifted higher and higher until it is floating at the same level as a large lake that forms part of the canal. When the gates of the last lock are opened, the ship sails across the lake and into another narrow channel. Three sets of locks in that channel lower the ship to the water level of the Pacific Ocean. Then the ship can continue its journey.

Now the United States government is thinking about building a new canal near the present Panama Canal, because the traffic through the Panama Canal is so great.

The locks of the Panama Canal let water in or out to raise or lower ships.

The Firth of Forth Bridge crosses a wide bay in Scotland.

The bridge over the Saint John River in New Brunswick, Canada,
is one of the longest covered bridges anywhere.

LINKS TO LAND

When you travel from place to place and rivers and lakes get in the way, you can go across by boat, or go around them, or go over a bridge. People build bridges to make it easier to travel from place to place.

The San Francisco-Oakland Bay Bridge crosses San Francisco Bay and connects the cities of San Francisco and Oakland, California. The Bay Bridge is a double-deck bridge. Both decks are used by cars, trucks, and buses.

The Firth of Forth Bridge in Scotland is a huge railroad bridge over the River Forth.

The Quebec Bridge in Canada is a railroad bridge that crosses the Saint Lawrence River.

The Mackinac Bridge links the Upper and Lower peninsulas of Michigan.

The Peace Bridge crosses the Niagara River between New York and Ontario. The bridge is a symbol of friendship between the United States and Canada.

One of the longest covered bridges in the world crosses the Saint John River in New Brunswick, Canada. It has a covered footwalk for pedestrians.

The longest pontoon, or floating, bridge crosses Lake Washington in Seattle, Washington.

A HIGHWAY OVER WATER

There is a highway in Louisiana that you can ride on for 24 miles (39 kilometers) and see nothing but water on both sides. It goes right across the middle of Lake Pontchartrain, the largest lake in Louisiana. Called the Lake Pontchartrain Causeway, it is the longest overwater highway in the world. The state of Louisiana built the causeway so that people would not have to drive all the way around this big lake.

What kind of place do you think is most fun? A place where you can ride a giant Ferris wheel? Or a place where you can ride in a boat down a jungle river? Or a place that makes you feel like a giant?

On the following pages, you will visit famous places of amusement that are in different parts of the world.

Shakespeare Memorial, Stratford-upon-Avon, England

PLAY TIME IN ENGLAND

Many people say that Shakespeare's poems and plays are the best ever written. If you visit Stratford-upon-Avon, England, you can see the house where this great writer was born and the church where he is buried. Nearby, you can visit the school he went to.

Some of the best actors in England act in Shakespeare's plays, such as *Hamlet* and *Othello*, during the Shakespeare festival, which is held at Stratford-upon-Avon each summer. Big audiences watch the plays in the theater of the Shakespeare Memorial, which was built more than two hundred years after Shakespeare died.

Years ago, the festival lasted for just one week. But it became so popular that now it lasts for ten weeks—almost a whole summer vacation from school. Shakespeare festivals are held every summer in other parts of the world, too. The United States has one in Stratford, Connecticut, and Shakespeare's plays are part of the yearly Stratford Festival in Stratford, Ontario, Canada.

Actors at the Shakespeare Memorial Theatre perform in Shakespeare's play, *Henry VIII*.

Opera lovers watch an opera performed at La Scala Opera House.

A HOUSE FOR SONGS

La Scala in Milan, Italy, is a house built for singing—an opera house. It is built on the same ground where the Church of Santa Maria della Scala once stood. The opera house is named for the same family as the church was.

An opera is a play told to music. The performers sing the parts they play. Sometimes they may talk, and sometimes they may even dance. What they do depends on the kind of opera it is.

Some of the most famous operas, such as *Madame Butterfly* by Puccini and *Falstaff* by Verdi, were first performed at La Scala. The world-famous director Arturo Toscanini once directed music there for such famous opera singers as Renata Tebaldi and Rosa Raisa.

La Scala is the most important opera house in Italy and one of the most famous opera houses in the world.

La Scala Opera House, Milan, Italy

Visitors can look through glass in the bottom of this boat as they cruise down the Weekiwachee River in Florida.

FUN ON WATER

In Weekiwachee Springs, Florida, you can be sort of an underwater explorer and not even get wet. The Weekiwachee River begins in Weekiwachee Springs. You can float down the Weekiwachee River in a boat that has a paddle wheel. You can see fish swim under the glass bottom of the boat. After the boat ride, you can see an underwater show and not get wet, either. You can go down into a theater where you can watch an underwater show in the river through a big sheet of glass that looks like a movie screen.

You can't see an underwater show in Xochimilco, Mexico. But you can see many small boats decorated with fresh flowers. And you can float on a boat down a canal that runs between the Floating Gardens of Lake Xochimilco. Indians guide the boats with long poles that they shove into the water.

Long ago, the Floating Gardens really floated. Aztec Indians built the gardens on the water with twigs and reeds covered with soil. Later, the roots of plants grew all the way down to the bottom of the lake and anchored the Floating Gardens.

Boats decorated with flowers carry passengers through a canal to the Floating Gardens of Lake Xochimilco, Mexico.

Every evening, the Chinese Pagoda restaurant
in the Tivoli is lighted.

The building in this picture is a concert hall
in the Tivoli in Copenhagen, Denmark.

CARNIVAL IN COPENHAGEN

Visitors to the Tivoli can ride
in a coach through the park.

In the daytime, the Tivoli in Copenhagen, Denmark, is a shady park where you can sail your toy boats during the summer on a peaceful lake. But, at night, the Tivoli turns into a kind of carnival. Trapeze artists, acrobats, and jugglers perform. Ballet dancers leap and spin on the stage of an open-air theater. Boats drift slowly across the lake, which is lighted with different colored lights. And, in the Children's Corner, you can take a ride on a tiny train.

On Saturdays, Sundays, and holidays, boys dress up as royal guards and march to band music right down the middle of the Tivoli. Later in the evening, the sky lights up with fireworks. But when morning comes, the Tivoli is again just a shady park.

THE MAGIC KINGDOM

How would you like to visit a fairy-tale castle? It's right out of the pages of the story, "Cinderella." This castle is in Walt Disney World in Florida—a place where the land of make-believe comes true.

Do you remember "Snow White and the Seven Dwarfs"? In the *Magic Kingdom* you might get a chance to shake hands with your favorite dwarf—be it Bashful, Doc, Dopey, Grumpy, Happy, Sleepy, or Sneezy. And of course you'll see Mickey and Minnie Mouse and all your other favorite Disney characters.

On *Main Street, U.S.A.,* you can climb aboard a fire engine that goes clanging away. You can ride in the open, upper deck of a double-deck bus. There's even a trolley pulled by a horse. And that's just the start of your traveling fun!

What's it like to fly to the moon? Find out in *Tomorrowland.* In *Frontierland* you can ride an Indian canoe or a riverboat. How about crossing over to *Tom Sawyer's Island* on a raft? Or, perhaps you'd like to cruise down a jungle river as lifelike animals move and roar in *Adventureland.*

What's all the screaming about? It's the *Mad Tea Party*, where giant cups and saucers spin you until you're dizzy. That puffing steam comes from a train that takes you for a trip around the *Magic Kingdom.* And the happy carnival music that fills the air comes from Cinderella's Golden Carrousel, where you have a choice of ninety galloping horses to ride.

There's still another *Magic Kingdom* in California. It's called Disneyland. This *Magic Kingdom* has many of the same rides and attractions as Walt Disney World in Florida.

Cinderella's castle rises high above
the Magic Kingdom that is Walt Disney World.

Which one of Walt Disney's Seven Dwarfs
would you like to meet in person?

THE BIG WHEEL OF VIENNA

Once, an Englishman wanted to build a big Ferris wheel as high as a twenty-storied building. He wanted it placed in a park called the Prater in Vienna, Austria. Safety engineers checked the plans for the huge Ferris wheel to make sure it would be safe. Then they told the Englishman that the wheel could be built. The men who made the parts tried to bring the huge axle to the place where the Ferris wheel would spin on it. But the axle was so big and heavy that it sank into the ground. Eight horses couldn't budge the axle. Sixteen horses couldn't budge it. Finally, the men managed to move the axle to the park on a special road of wooden planks. It was such a special Ferris wheel, that when it was nearly finished, the builders let the wife of a British ambassador fasten the last bolt. Now, the giant Ferris wheel was ready. But, the question was, would it work? Slowly, slowly, the giant wheel began to spin. It worked! It was safe!

If you visit the Prater today, you can ride up, up, up, as high as a twenty-storied building, in the biggest Ferris wheel in the world. The name of the Englishman, who planned and had it built in Vienna long ago, was Walter Basset.

THE LAND OF LILLIPUT

In the book *Gulliver's Travels,* by Jonathan Swift, Gulliver visits Lilliput, a land of tiny people. Gulliver is an ordinary-sized man. But to the Lilliputians, he looks like a giant!

You can imagine how Gulliver felt if you visit Madurodam, a miniature city in The Hague in The Netherlands. Everything in Madurodam is twenty-five times smaller than real life. You can reach down to touch ships in the harbor or reach up to cover a lighthouse beacon with your hand. You can leap across canals and race express trains through the countryside.

Cars hum below you as you walk beside modern highways. You tower over cows and windmills. If you put your ear to the church or the opera house, you hear music. At night, the little city quiets down. Then lights go on in the houses and on the streets. At the airport, tower lights sweep the sky.

There's a bronze plaque at the entrance to Madurodam. It shows George Maduro, a hero of The Netherlands who died in World War II. Maduro's parents built the miniature city in his memory—a place to be enjoyed by all, but especially by children.

336

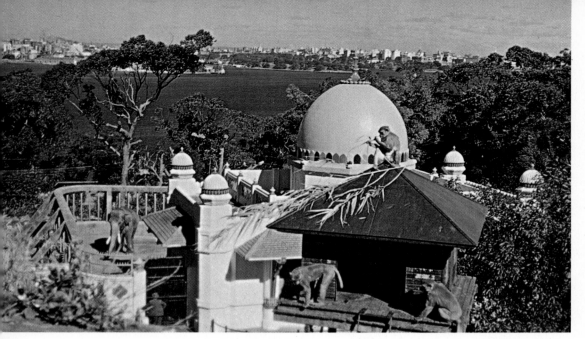

The Taronga Park Zoo, Sydney, Australia

ZOOS AROUND THE WORLD

It's hard to get close to a wild animal. Some animals might charge you the way a rhinoceros does, and you would have to scramble to get away. Other animals, like the giraffe, run away from you so fast that you barely get a look at them. Still other animals are so rare that they are hard to find—such as the giant turtle. But you can see all these animals and many more, if you go to a zoo. And not only that, but in a zoo the animals are all safely behind bars or fences or moats, so you can watch them all you want. In some zoos, you can even feed the animals.

There are zoos in nearly every country in the world. Some zoos have special features that make them different from others. For example, the Biblical Zoo in Jerusalem, Israel, has many animals that are mentioned in the Bible. The San Diego Zoo in California has the largest collection of animals anywhere. And the nearby San Diego Wild Animal Park has more land—1,800 acres (728 hectares)—than any other zoo.

The Biblical Zoo, Jerusalem, Israel

The Bronx Zoo, New York City

HONG KONG ISLAND GARDEN

Up, up, up you go in a cable car for a breathtaking ride to Victoria Peak. That's the highest point on Hong Kong island, off the south coast of China. From the cable-car stop, you can travel by bus or car to the Tiger Balm Gardens.

There are no tigers in the Tiger Balm Gardens. This fantastic place was built by a rich man named Aw Boon Haw, who made his fortune selling a medicine called Tiger Balm. The gardens are full of weird statues of animals and men. There also are statues of characters from Chinese legends. And topping it all is a beautiful seven-story white pagoda, or tower.

You don't have to pay to get into the Tiger Balm Gardens. And while you are visiting the gardens, you can also get a pass to see a priceless collection of jade in the founder's family home, which is in the park.

From the gardens, you can look down on Happy Valley, the island's sports center. In fall and winter, crowds gather there to enjoy horse racing, field hockey, soccer, and other sports.

WALL OF CHINA

JERICHO

TAXCO

Would you like to visit places that are really different—places where you can see a tower that tips, or the oldest city in the world, or the world's longest front porch?

The next few pages will tell you about some of the queer, quaint, and curious places in many different parts of the world.

THE FALLING TOWER

You can see a bell tower that leans in the town of Pisa, Italy. What does it lean against? Nothing.

It's called the Leaning Tower of Pisa, and it's been leaning more and more ever since it was built about 700 years ago. Some say that long ago the great Italian scientist Galileo dropped weights from the tower to learn how fast things fall. Even then, the tower was a leaning tower.

And today, little by little, one side of the tower keeps on sinking into the soft ground. The Leaning Tower tips about an inch every nine years. The farther it leans out of line the faster it tips.

You can climb stairs to the top of the tower and see the bells that once called people to a nearby church. But no one rings the bells now. The clanging might make the tower fall faster.

The government of Italy once offered a prize for the best plan to keep the tower from falling any farther. Some people have ideas, but nothing has been done yet.

If the Leaning Tower ever falls, it will be the end of what some people say is one of the seven wonders of the modern world.

This building, called the Atomium, was made for the World's Fair in Brussels, Belgium, in 1958.

STRANGE PLACES TO EAT IN

Everything, including the food you eat, is made up of invisible specks called atoms. You could never eat inside an atom—anyone knows that. It would be much too small.

But in Brussels, Belgium, you can do the next best thing—at a place called the Atomium. You can eat inside a model of an atom. The model is hundreds of billions of times as big as a real atom.

The Atomium is a model of a clump of atoms called a molecule. It is higher than a thirty-storied building, and each of the round steel balls is a model of an atom. Inside the ball at the top is a restaurant.

You can ride a moving staircase from one ball to another until you get to the restaurant. Or you can swoosh straight up to the restaurant in one of the fastest elevators in Europe.

In the United States, you can eat dinner even higher off the ground. You can ride in an elevator twice as high as the Atomium to the restaurant on top of the Space Needle in Seattle, Washington. You get an extra ride in the Space Needle. The restaurant at the top turns on its center—once every hour.

Both the Atomium and the Space Needle were built for world's fairs.

The Space Needle, in Seattle, Washington, was built for the Seattle World's Fair of 1962.

AND THE WALLS
CAME TUMBLIN' DOWN

The Bible tells the story of a great battle in which Joshua, a leader of the Jews, made his people shout and blow on rams' horns until the walls of Jericho came tumbling down.

In those days, Jericho was a great city. But today you see only a big heap of dirt near the Dead Sea in the country once called Palestine.

This mound of earth is all that's left of what may be the oldest city in the world. By digging down through layer after layer of earth and stones, scientists have found parts of the walls of nearly thirty cities piled one on top of the other.

Nobody can tell which one of these walls was brought down by the shouts of the Jews. But the scientists are learning a lot about what may be the oldest city in the world.

Scientists have dug holes in Jordan to find the Jericho Walls.

This drawing shows priests carrying the sacred Ark of the Covenant while the walls of Jericho fall.

THE HOUSE THAT ALEX BUILT

One day, a man named Alex Jordan was wandering around a hilly countryside in Wisconsin, when he saw a huge rock. It was as tall as a thirty-story skyscraper, and it was shaped like a giant chimney. He was filled with wonder when he saw the rock because rocks and stones meant something special to him. He was a sculptor. A sculptor carves things out of stone.

He climbed to the top of the rock and thought, "What a perfect place for a quiet workshop, away from the city." So, he decided to build a one-room shop on top. He gathered his tools and building equipment together and started work.

When his shop was finished, he was so pleased that he added more rooms to his shop. Then it began to look like a house. Wherever he could, he used the rock as part of his house. Instead of chipping away the rock, he used it as a wall, a stairstep, or as part of a fireplace. And instead of cutting down the trees that grew on the rock, he built the rooms around the trees, leaving holes in the roof for them to poke through.

Today, the house is called *The House on the Rock*, and hundreds of people take special trips to Wisconsin to see Mr. Jordan's house.

S.M.O.M.

Is S.M.O.M. the smallest country in the world? Some say it is but others don't count it at all. Small country or not, it has a long name—the Sovereign and Military Order of Saint John of Jerusalem, Rhodes, and Malta. It's called S.M.O.M. for short.

The people of S.M.O.M. are called Knights, and they are ruled by a grand master. Once S.M.O.M. had lands in many parts of the world, but now S.M.O.M. has only three fine old buildings in Rome, Italy.

One of these buildings, the Villa dei Cavalieri, has one of the most beautiful views in Rome. If you peek through the peephole of a great wooden door at the villa, you can see the dome of Saint Peter's Church.

If you do, you may be looking at three countries—Italy, S.M.O.M., and the Vatican.

This is the Villa dei Cavalieri, the headquarters of S.M.O.M.

Through a peephole in the front door of the Villa dei Cavalieri, you can see the dome of Saint Peter's Church.

THE EIFFEL OF PARIS

Do you know where you can get an "eyeful" of Paris? From the top of the Eiffel Tower, of course.

But the name and the view only sound alike. The Eiffel Tower is named for Alexandre Eiffel, a great French engineer. Mr. Eiffel built this first skyscraper of them all before your grandparents were born.

France decided to have a fair to show off its finest goods, and wares, and machinery. The people of France wanted the fair to have something extra special in the middle of the fairgrounds, and Alexandre Eiffel was picked to build it.

When the iron beams and bolts started to rise, many people did not like the tower. They called it a gigantic skeleton. But when it was finished and lighted up at night, they changed their minds. It looked like a tower of lace.

If you take an elevator a hundred stories up to the top of the tower, not only can you see the city of Paris, but you can buy a hot dog from the highest hot-dog stand in the world.

But even without leaving your room in Paris, you can get an "eyeful" from the Eiffel Tower. The Eiffel Tower has a TV antenna that sends television programs all over Paris. Some people count the Eiffel Tower as one of the seven wonders of the modern world.

352

Some people climb steps to the top of the Eiffel Tower for a view of Paris.

There's an island in the United States between Lake Huron and Lake Michigan that's still in the horse and buggy days. The most important traffic law on Mackinac Island is NO CARS ALLOWED.

NO
CARS
ALLOWED

As your steamer pulls in to the dock at Mackinac Island, you can see rows of brightly painted carriages. As soon as you get off the boat, you can pick out a horse and buggy and ride around in it to see the island's many sights.

In your horse and buggy, you can visit Sugar Loaf Rock or the Devil's Kitchen, where the wind and waves have carved tunnels and caves. The Indians thought these were the homes of Great Spirits.

You can visit old Fort Mackinac, where British and American soldiers once fought to control the Northwest Territory.

You can visit John Jacob Astor's fur post, where trappers and Indians once brought millions of dollars' worth of animal skins each spring.

And you can watch yachts and speedboats in the harbor from the front porch of the Grand Hotel—the longest front porch in the world.

The blockhouse of the Old Fort Mackinac overlooks part of Mackinac Island.

The Grand Hotel on Mackinac Island is one of the largest summer hotels in the world.

People travel by horse or bicycle on Mackinac Island.

WHAT A WALL!

In China, there is a wall that twists and turns like a dragon as it goes over mountains and across valleys. It is about as high as a three-story building. And it goes on and on, for more than 1,500 miles (2,410 kilometers). No wonder it is called the Great Wall of China!

At one time, there were many rulers in China. These rulers often put up walls to protect their land and their people. About two thousand years ago, the first emperor of all China decided to connect some of these walls. He wanted to protect China from invaders living to the north. So he began work on the Great Wall. It was made of dirt, stones, and bricks. And the top was wide enough for troops and horsemen to use as a road.

In later years, other emperors made repairs and added new sections to the wall. The last work was done about four hundred years ago. Much of the Great Wall still stands. But it isn't any good for protection because airplanes can fly over it.

357

Illustration Acknowledgments

The publishers of *Childcraft* gratefully acknowledge the following artists, photographers, publishers, agencies, and corporations for illustrations in this volume. Page numbers refer to two-page spreads. The words *"(left)," "(center)," "(top)," "(bottom),"* and *"(right),"* indicate position on the spread. All illustrations are the exclusive property of the publishers of *Childcraft* unless names are marked with an asterisk (*).

1: Robert Keys
4-5: Fred Steffen
6-17: © 1962 by Sawyer's Inc. *
18-19: *(left)* © 1962 by Sawyer's Inc. *; *(right)* Fred Steffen
20-21: *(top)* James R. Simon, Van Cleve Photography *; *(bottom)* Loren McIntyre, Woodfin Camp, Inc. *
22-23: A. L. Goldman, Rapho Guillumette *
24-25: Icelandic Photo & Press Service *
26-27: FPG *
28-29: Earl Kubis, Tom Stack & Assoc. *
30-31: Paul Popper *
32-33: *(left)* Walter Romanes *; *(right)* L. W. Swan *
34-35: *Childcraft* photo
36-37: *(left)* Ed Drews, Photo Researchers *; *(right)* *Childcraft* photo, Jerry Frank, DPI *
38-39: *(left)* Emil Schulthess *; *(right)* Fred Steffen
40-41: *(left)* Julian Caraballo, Tom Stack & Assoc. *; *(right)* McMullin, Pictorial Parade *
42-43: *(left)* Shostal *; *(right)* National Film Board of Canada *
44-45: *(left)* Fox Photos, Ltd. *; *(right)* Ray Manley, Shostal *
46-47: Shostal *
48-49: *(left)* Everett Johnson, DeWys, Inc. *; *(right)* Porterfield-Chickering from Artstreet *
50-51: *(left)* Camera Press, Pix *; *(right)* Kjell Johansson from Carl Ostman *
52-53: George Hall, Woodfin Camp, Inc. *
54-55: *(left)* Japan National Tourist Office *; *(right)* I. Umeyama *
56-57: *(left)* Kronfeld, FPG *; *(right)* *Childcraft* photo
58-59: *(left)* Bernheim, Pictorial Parade. Courtesy, Frederick Kiesler and Armand Bartos, Architects *; *(right)* Fred Steffen
60-61: *(left)* Pictorial Parade *; *(right)* Basilica di S. Petro, Rome (Alinari from Art Reference Bureau) *
62-63: Photo Trends *
64-65: Paolo Koch, Rapho Guillumette *
66-67: *(left)* Shostal *; *(right)* Monkmeyer *
68-69: Bavaria Verlag *
70-71: Lorin D. Wiggins *
72-73: Mercer Sullivan, FPG *
74-75: *(top)* Three Lions *; *(bottom)* Ed Drews, Photo Researchers *
76-77: *(left)* Shostal *; *(top right)* Bernard G. Silbestein *; *(bottom right)* Shostal *
78-79: David Rubinger, Black Star *
80-81: *(left)* *Childcraft* photo by Don Stebbing; *(right)* George Suyeoka
82-83: *(left)* Fritz Henle, Monkmeyer *; *(top right)* Lawrence Smith, Photo Researchers *; *(center right)* D. Jordan Wilson, Pix *; *(bottom right)* Shostal *
84-85: *(top, left to right)* Fritz Henle, Photo Researchers *, Ruth Block, Pictorial Parade *, C. A. Peterson, Rapho Guillumette *; *(bottom, left to right)* Deller, Monkmeyer *, Griffin, FPG *
86-87: *(left to right)* Ken Lambert, FPG *, Berger, FPG *, Shostal *
88-89: *(left)* *Childcraft* photo; *(right)* Pix *
90-91: *(left)* Camera Clix *; *(right)* French Government Tourist Bureau *

92-93: Paul Conklin *
94-95: *(left)* Mansell Collection *; *(right)* Shostal *
96-97: T. Irie *
98-99: *Childcraft* photos
100-101: *(left)* Michael Manheim *; *(right)* Shelbee Matis
102-103: *(left)* Graham Woodmansterne *; *(right)* Louis Goldman, Rapho Guillumette *
104-105: *(left)* Madeline Grimoldi *; *(right)* Italian State Tourist Office *
106-107: *(left)* *Childcraft* photo; *(right)* Elliot Erwitt, Magnum *
108-109: *(top, left to right)* Pictorial Parade *, The British Travel Association *, Henle, Photo Researchers *; *(bottom)* Schalek, Three Lions *
110-111: *(left)* Ray Manley, Shostal *; *(right)* by permission of H. M. The Queen, Windsor Castle *
112-113: Air Photo Service *
114-115: *(left)* United Press Int. *; *(right)* Wide World *
116-117: Orion Press from Stock, Boston *
118-119: *(left)* Marvin Newman, Woodfin Camp, Inc. *; *(right)* Shelbee Matis
120-121: *(left)* Frank, DPI *; *(right)* Three Lions *
122-123: Björn Bölstad from Peter Arnold *
124-125: *(top)* Brian Blake, Rapho Guillumette *; *(bottom)* Richard Harrington, Three Lions *
126-127: *(left)* David Forbert, Monkmeyer *; *(right)* Carl Purcell *
128-129: *(left)* Photo Researchers *; *(right)* Denver & Rio Grande Western R.R. *
130-131: *(left)* Bill Noel Kleeman, Tom Stack & Assoc. *; *(right)* J. Alex Langley, DPI *
132-133: *(left)* Uffizi Gallery, Florence (Alinari from Art Reference Bureau) *; *(right)* Stern, Monkmeyer *
134-135: *(left)* Frances Mortimer, Rapho Guillumette *; *(right)* Ted Bumiller, Monkmeyer *
136-137: Klaus Schnitzer, DPI *
138-139: *(left)* Three Lions *; *(right)* Fred Steffen
140-141: G. R. Roberts *
142-143: *(left)* Three Lions *; *(right)* Monkmeyer *
144-145: Doug Morris, Barnaby's Picture Library *
146-147: *(left)* Shostal *; *(right)* Georgia Dept. of Commerce *
148-149: *(left)* The British Travel Association *; *(right)* Arnold Newman, © Curtis Publishing Co. *
150-151: Dick Kent *
152-153: Robert H. Glaze, Artstreet *
154-155: J. D. Raymond
156-157: *(left)* Three Lions *; *(right)* Fred Steffen
158-159: *(left)* Gorter, Pix *; *(right)* Gendreau *
160-161: *(left)* TWA *; *(right)* Shostal *
162-163: George Holton, Photo Researchers *
164-165: *(left)* Monkmeyer *; *(right)* Historical Pictures Service *
166-167: Takayuki Toyama, Orion Press *
168-169: *(left)* Ray Manley, Shostal *; *(right)* Historical Pictures Service *
170-171: *Childcraft* photo
172-173: *(left)* Laurence Lowry, Rapho Guillumette *; *(right)* Eric M. Sanford *
174-175: *(left)* Kidson, Pix *; *(right)* George Suyeoka
176-177: *(left)* *Childcraft* photo; *(right)* De Beers Consolidated Mines, Ltd. *
178-179: *(left)* Margaret Brandow, Tom Stack & Assoc. *; *(right)* H. Friesteat from Carl Ostman *
180-181: David Moore, Black Star *
182-183: *(left)* Fujihira, Monkmeyer *; *(right)* Evans, Three Lions *
184-185: *(left)* *Childcraft* photo; *(right)* USDA *
186-187: M. Vital, *Paris Match*
188-189: John Running, Stock, Boston *
190-191: Pictorial Parade *
192-193: *(left)* Herbert Lanks, Black Star *; *(right)* Fred Steffen
194-195: *(left)* World Photo Service from Madeline Grimoldi *; *(right)* Marc and Evelyne Bernheim, Rapho Guillumette *
196-197: *(left)* Tom Dolan; *(right)* *Childcraft* photos by J. R. Eyerman
198-199: *(left)* Pellegrini from Madeline Grimoldi *; *(right)* J. Alex Langley, DPI
200-201: *(left)* Jerry Frank, DPI *; *(right)* Frank Siteman, Stock, Boston *
202-203: *(left)* Leni Sonnenfeld, Pictorial Parade *; *(right)* Daniel, Pix *

204-205: Rapho Guillumette *
206-207: (left) British Information Services *; (right) USDA *
208-209: (left) Photographic Library of Australia *; (right) Warren Garst *
210-211: (left) Russ Kinne, Photo Researchers *; (right) George Suyeoka
212-213: Mauritius-Verlag from Van Cleve Photography *
214-215: (left) Three Lions *; (right) Alinari from Art Reference Bureau *
216-217: (left to right) Fritz Henle, Monkmeyer *, Engelhard, Monkmeyer *, Childcraft photo, Ursula Mahoney, Pictorial Parade *
218-219: (left) Brazilian Government Trade Bureau *; (right) Litwin, Photo Researchers *
220-221: (left) Louis Slobodkin; (right) Swiss National Tourist Office *
222-223: (left) Pictorial Parade *; (right) Shostal *
224-225: (left) Childcraft photo; (right) Guy Flatley, Monkmeyer *
226-227: Stone Mountain Memorial Association *
228-229: (top) Kentucky Dept. of Public Information *; (bottom, left to right) Eastern Photo Service *, Ray E. White *, Three Lions *
230-231: (left) John Mathisen *; (right) Fred Steffen
232-233: Al Geise, Pictorial Parade *
234-235: (top) Childcraft photo; (bottom) I. Holmsen, from Carl Ostman
236-237: (top left) Laurenza, UNESCO *; (bottom left) Gunter Reitz, Pix *; (right) Weber, Three Lions *
238-239: (left) Laurence Lowry, Rapho Guillumette *; (right) Aigner, Monkmeyer *
240-241: Kronfeld, FPG *
242-243: William M. Graham, Photo Researchers *
244-245: Bob and Ira Spring *
246-247: (left) Ken Lambert, Pix *; (right) Ken Lambert, Pictorial Parade *
248-249: (left) Joe Rychetnik, Photo Researchers *; (right) Fred Steffen
250-251: R. Christopher, Pix *
252-253: (left) Childcraft photo; (right) Alan Band Associates *
254-255: Childcraft photo by Edward F. Hoppe
256-257: (left) Henle, Monkmeyer *; (right) Shostal *
258-259: Jacques Jangoux
260-261: Adam Woolfitt, Woodfin Camp, Inc. *
262-263: Franklin McMahon
264-265: (left) United Press Int. *; (right) A. L. Goldman, Rapho Guillumette *
266-267: Franklin McMahon
268-269: (left) Björn Bölstad from Peter Arnold *; (right) Fred Steffen
270-271: (left) Culver *; (right) San Antonio Chamber of Commerce
272-273: (top) Robert Capa, Magnum, Life, © Time Inc. *; (bottom) Almasy, Three Lions *
274-275: (left) Shostal *; (right) George Holton, Photo Researchers *
276-277: Brown Brothers *
278-279: (left) Museum of Fine Arts, Houston, The Hogg Brothers Collection *; (right) Rena, Pix *
280-281: Permission by Trustees of the British Museum (Art Reference Bureau) *
282-283: FPG *
284-285: (left) Prescotts' History of Mexico *; (right) Childcraft photo by John Wolff
286-287: (left) United Press Int. *; (right) Fred Steffen
288-289: (top left) Colonial Williamsburg *; (bottom left) Peter Roll, Photo Researchers *; (right) Three Lions *

290-291: (left) Wide World *; (right) The Interior of the Pantheon by Panini, The National Gallery of Art, Washington, D.C., S. H. Kress Collection *
292-293: (left) Fred Maroon *; (right) Shannon Free Airport Development Co. *
294-295: (left) Calvin D. Campbell, Pictorial Parade *; (right) U.S. Navy *
296-297: Uni Photos *
298-299: Bob Taylor *
300-301: (left) Jane Latta, Photo Researchers *; (right) Three Lions *
302-303: (left) Bradley Smith *, Photo Researchers *; (right) Weinberger, Alpha
304-305: Commonwealth of Puerto Rico *
306-307: (left) Childcraft photo by Don Stebbing; (right) Fred Steffen
308-309: (left) Culver *; (right) State of California, Department of Public Works *
310-311: (left) Shostal *; (right) Kronfeld, FPG *;
312-313: (top left) Folger Shakespeare Library * (bottom left) G. F. Allen, Pix *; (right) Lake Havasu City, Arizona *
314-315: (top) French National Railroads *; (bottom) Bettmann Archive *
316-317: (left) Leni Sonnenfeld, Pictorial Parade *; (right) Stephanie Dinkins, Shostal *
318-319: (top left) Wide World *; (bottom left) Rapho Guillumette *; (right) Wide World *
320-321: (top) FPG *; (bottom) New Brunswick Travel Bureau *
322-323: (left) Industrial Photography, Inc. *; (right) Fred Steffen
324-325: (left) Shostal *; (right) Tom Hollyman, Photo Researchers *
326-327: (left) Three Lions *; (right) Childcraft photo
328-329: (left) Weekiwachee Springs, Florida *; (right) Childcraft photo
330-331: (left) George Holton, Photo Researchers *; (top right) Bernard Silberstein, Rapho Guillumette *; (bottom right) Shostal *
332-333: Fred Ward, Black Star *
334-335: Three Lions *
336-337: Björn Bölstad from Peter Arnold *
338-339: (left) Childcraft photo; (top right) Israel Press & Photo Agency *; (bottom right) New York Convention & Visitors Bureau *
340-341: (left) Robert H. Glaze, Artstreet *; (right) Fred Steffen
342-343: (left) Walter Scott, FPG *; (right) Ernest Nash, Three Lions *
344-345: (left) John P. Taylor, Rapho Guillumette *; (right) Earl Scott, Photo Researchers *
346-347: (left) Culver *; (right) Richard Hufnagle, Publix *
348-349: G. B. Telfair, House on the Rock, Inc. *
350-351: Giordani
352-353: (left to right) Monkmeyer *, Childcraft photo, John Ross, Photo Researchers *
354-355: (top to bottom) Wide World *, Three Lions *, Monkmeyer *
356-357: Tomaya, Black Star *

Heritage binding cover—(left to right): (back) © Sawyer's Inc. *, Photographic Library of Australia *, Franklin McMahon, Childcraft photo; (spine) Childcraft photo; (front) Childcraft photo, Tor Eigeland *, Childcraft photo, Childcraft photo

Index

This index is an alphabetical list of the important topics covered in this book. It will help you find information given in both words *and* pictures. To help you understand what an entry means, there is often a helping word in parentheses. For example, **gargoyles** (statues). If there is information in both words and pictures, you will see the words *with pictures* after the page number. If there is *only* a picture, you will see the word *picture* before the page number. If you do not find what you want in this index, please go to the General Index in Volume 15, which is a key to all of the books.